Under Grace Hamman's tutelage, readers enter a "school of love." *Jesus through Medieval Eyes* challenges our assumptions about Jesus, expanding our vision of him with medieval images. After reading this book, we know Jesus as judge, lover, mother, and more. Contrary to books that offer contemporary solutions to contemporary problems, *Jesus through Medieval Eyes* illuminates an eternal and timeless Savior.

> **Jessica Hooten Wilson,** Fletcher Jones Endowed Chair of Great Books at Pepperdine University, author of *Reading for the Love of God*

In *Jesus Through Medieval Eyes* Grace Hamman combines the scholarly and the practical in a way that is, alas, all too uncommon. She deploys her broad and deep knowledge of the Middle Ages in the service of helping ordinary Christians become more knowledgeable and more faithful lovers of Christ. Beautifully and engagingly written, this book helps us understand ourselves better by introducing us to our fellow Christians who lived in a world that is at once strikingly strange and strangely familiar.

> **Fritz Bauerschmidt,** professor of theology, Loyola University Maryland; deacon of the Archdiocese of Baltimore

Jesus Through Medieval Eyes offers vivid, earthy, and sometimes jarring insights into Jesus as seen through the lives and minds of those who walked this faith journey ahead of us. The Jesus they understood is, in some ways, as startling to us as our portrayals of him today would be to them. But we have much to learn from ages past, and Grace Hamman is the perfect one to guide us on this tour. Her writing is as sharp, witty, and sparkling as the medieval minds she studies and introduces us to. This book is rich and utterly delightful.

> **Karen Swallow Prior,** PhD, author of *The Evangelical Imagination: How Stories, Images & Metaphors Created a Culture in Crisis*

With a scholar's eye and a pastor's hand, Grace Hamman gently accompanies us on a journey of challenging our under-examined beliefs and biases until we find ourselves beholding Christ in new, exciting ways. This book is a breath of fresh air.

Shannon K. Evans, author *of Rewilding Motherhood*
and *Feminist Prayers for My Daughter*

In *Jesus through Medieval Eyes*, Grace Hamman offers an absorbing and accessible work of Christian retrieval, guiding readers back to the delightfully distinct treasures of medieval Christianity. With erudition and devotional care, Hamman guides us toward the radiant goodness of Christ—a goodness best beheld when we gaze upon him from a vantage point beyond our own. Whether "medieval" as a modifier to "Christianity" makes you sing with joy, hum with curiosity, or shriek with fear, humble readers will find this book an intellectual and spiritual feast.

Claude Atcho, pastor of Church of the Resurrection,
author of *Reading Black Books*

Jesus through Medieval Eyes

Jesus through Medieval Eyes

Beholding Christ with the
Artists, Mystics, and Theologians
of the Middle Ages

Grace Hamman

ZONDERVAN
REFLECTIVE

ZONDERVAN REFLECTIVE

Jesus through Medieval Eyes
Copyright © 2023 by Grace Hamman

Requests for information should be addressed to:
Zondervan, *3900 Sparks Dr. SE, Grand Rapids, Michigan 49546*

Zondervan titles may be purchased in bulk for educational, business, fundraising, or sales promotional use. For information, please email SpecialMarkets@Zondervan.com.

ISBN 978-0-310-14585-1 (audio)

Library of Congress Cataloging-in-Publication Data

Names: Hamman, Grace, author.
Title: Jesus through medieval eyes : beholding Christ with the artists, mystics, and theologians of the Middle Ages / Grace Hamman.
Description: Grand Rapids : Zondervan, 2023.
Identifiers: LCCN 2023013026 (print) | LCCN 2023013027 (ebook) | ISBN 9780310145837 (hardcover) | ISBN 9780310145844 (ebook)
Subjects: LCSH: Jesus Christ—History of doctrines—Middle Ages, 600–1500. | Jesus Christ—Iconography. | Art, Medieval. | Literature, Medieval. | BISAC: RELIGION / Christianity / Literature & the Arts | RELIGION / Christian Living / Personal Growth
Classification: LCC BT198 .H359 2023 (print) | LCC BT198 (ebook) | DDC 232—dc23/eng/20230512
LC record available at https://lccn.loc.gov/2023013026
LC ebook record available at https://lccn.loc.gov/2023013027

Cover design: Darren Welch Design
Cover image: Bibliothèque nationale de France; Paseven / iStockphoto
Interior design: Kait Lamphere

Printed in the United States of America
23 24 25 26 27 LBC 5 4 3 2 1

For my beloved grandparents:
John and Carol
Ilene and Gerald

Contents

Foreword

The airplane was small—a puddle jumper, as my dad would say. It was March 2000, just a few months into the new millennium. The world had survived the nonevent of Y2K, and I had survived my PhD coursework. I would shortly submit my dissertation prospectus and sit for comprehensive exams, which explains why I was working even as I flew for a short vacation in Washington, DC. Several brown volumes, spines branded with the telling initials (telling to graduate students like me, that is) EETS—Early English Text Society—poked from the book bag at my feet.

I held one of the volumes open in my lap. I still remember reading the printed Middle English words, bouncing slightly from the rhythm of the flight. It was an *exempla* (sermon story) from John Mirk's *Festial*, a collection of late fourteenth-century Middle English sermons that became a fifteenth-century bestseller. This story told of a woman filled with despair over a "horrible" sin she had once committed. One night, Jesus appeared to her in a vision. Gently taking her hand, he placed it in the wound on his side. "My daughter," he said to her. "Why are you afraid to show me your heart as I have shown mine to you?" The next morning, when the woman awoke, she found her hand black with the blood of Christ. With newfound courage (and motivation from her bloody hand), she went to church, confessed her long-hidden sin to a priest, and watched her own personal miracle as her hand immediately became clean.

I stared at the story, mesmerized. A woman had personally met Jesus, and his intervention saved her. For the past three years I had been studying medieval Christianity. I understood the significance of saints such as Margaret of Antioch and Brigid of Kildare. I understood the beauty of Eucharist theology. I understood the comforting, and instructive, appeal of liturgy. I could even explain to my students how sacramental theology emerged.

But it wasn't until that moment, on a plane in March 2000, that I met the medieval Jesus. Instead of seeing him through the eyes of a Baptist protestant, I saw him through the eyes of a medieval woman. I saw him through the words of a medieval priest. And I realized that as different as my modern faith was from the world of medieval Christians, the Jesus we knew was the same.

This is the gift Grace Hamman has given us—in a world more prone to forget history than remember it, the beauty of her writing and the breadth of her knowledge help us see the rich complexity of a faith both strange and different from our own. Most importantly, by helping us understand how medieval people saw Jesus, she helps us better see Jesus too.

Beth Allison Barr

Acknowledgments

This book is rooted in many voices of wisdom. All errors are mine, but all graces and beauty bloom from the gifts of love and intellectual companionship that others have poured into me.

I am thankful for the hard work and guidance of the team at Zondervan Reflective, including Lex, Jesse, Kim, and Jeanine. A heartfelt thank-you is especially due to my editor, Kyle Rohane, whose enthusiasm, thoughtfulness, and vision for the project deeply encouraged me.

My agent, Keely Boeving, has been a skilled and wise book midwife guiding me through the labors and unexpected surprises of publication. I am really thankful for her friendship too.

To learn from sharp, insightful scholars is a gift. My professors at Duke did more than teach the discipline of reading medieval literature; they also modeled how love of the books themselves should change and challenge you. I learned to love and question medieval poetry and theology in conversations and classrooms with my brilliant advisor, David Aers. Sarah Beckwith graciously taught me that writing and thinking are inseparable. I am also thankful for the kindness and wisdom of Denise Baker.

Medievalist friends and longtime writing group members Jessica Hines and Jessica Ward read the majority of this book in various drafts. I am grateful for their keen minds, love of Middle English, and generous hearts. Goodwyn Bell also read certain versions. Her faithful pastoral instinct, perceptive questions, and friendship have been gifts in writing and beyond.

I have been blessed in friendship with some astounding women. Samantha Kingma, Chelsea Swanson, Donica Revere, Lindsey Larre, and Marisa Tualla all believed in me and encouraged my strange interests in moments when I found it hard to believe in myself. I hope they all see a bit of themselves in here—each has shaped my habits of love and thought. Thank you also to the Monday night small group members who patiently listened as I wrestled with what I actually believed about some of these medieval ideas.

My parents, John and Gayla, first taught me to love Jesus and to hold myself open to transformation. I can't describe how thankful I am for their witness and care. My mother-in-law, Christie, has generously and kindly flown in to save the day, feed us all, and take care of my children repeatedly in this process. My father-in-law, Randy, passed away shortly before I started writing this book, but I think about him every day as his faithful love continues to bear fruit in the life of my husband. My dear grandparents, John and Carol, model the beauty that unfolds when the love of learning and the love of God shape your life for almost one hundred years. My grandmother Ilene's faithfulness and creativity inspire me. I deeply love and am inspired by the character, strength, and delight of my siblings, John, Anna, and her husband, Austin.

Thank you to my children, Margaret, Simon, and Constance, whose joy in play, abundant love, and blessed neediness remind me who I am. Most of all, I thank my husband, Scott. Without his vision, faith, courage, and much-needed sense of humor, this book would have gone nowhere. How thankful I am to seek the face of Christ alongside you.

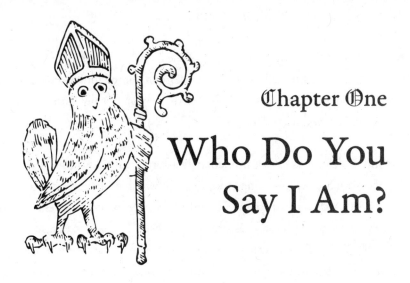

Chapter One

Who Do You Say I Am?

Who do you say I am? Christ's question to his disciples, recorded in three of the gospels, resounds through the ages right down to us. The way we answer Christ's query determines our beliefs and inflects how we live our lives. Father Greg Boyle argues that "nothing is more consequential in our lives than the notion of God we hold."[1] The question appears straightforward, but the gospel of Matthew shows us that it's surprisingly tricky and complicated.

When Jesus asks this question, Simon Peter answers with the candor and enthusiasm we expect of him:

> Now when Jesus came into the district of Caesarea Philippi, he asked his disciples, "Who do people say that the Son of Man is?" And they said, "Some say John the Baptist but others Elijah and still others Jeremiah or one of the prophets." He said to them, "But who do you say that I am?" Simon Peter answered,

---

1. Gregory Boyle, *The Whole Language: The Power of Extravagant Tenderness* (New York: Avid Reader, 2021), 1.

"You are the Messiah, the Son of the living God." And Jesus answered him, "Blessed are you, Simon son of Jonah! For flesh and blood has not revealed this to you but my Father in heaven." (Matt. 16:13–17)

Simon Peter gets it. But immediately after he answers that Jesus is Messiah, Son of the living God, Peter shows that he has crammed the Messiah into his own cultural ideals: He expects a Messiah who will triumphantly restore the power of Israel, not one who will die on a Roman cross. He argues that surely the Savior of the world would not suffer death and humiliation. Jesus says, "Get behind me, Satan!"

Peter, who gave the best possible answer to Jesus's question, was still human, with all of humanity's limitation of vision, even when encountering Jesus in the flesh back in first-century Palestine. Today we have a further barrier when we struggle to answer Christ's question for ourselves. We have not met Christ face-to-face, and the time and place in which we live limit our conception of him.

Henry Vaughan, the seventeenth-century Welsh poet, wrote a poem on John 3:2, when Nicodemus seeks out Jesus at nighttime. Vaughan describes Nicodemus:

> Most blest believer he!
> Who in that land of darkness and blind eyes
> Thy long-expected healing wings could see,
>   When Thou didst rise!
> And, what can never more be done,
> Did at midnight speak with the Sun![2]

---

2. Henry Vaughan, "The Night," in *Sacred Poems by Henry Vaughan with a Memoir by the Rev. H. F. Lyte* (London: G. Bell and Sons, 1914), 211–12. Spelling slightly updated by myself.

Nicodemus had crept out to hear Jesus in person. At night, without the omnipresent crowds, Jesus had shared with him in personal conversation. Vaughan puns in that last sentence. It is impossible to speak with the Sun at midnight. And with perhaps some rare exceptions of seers, mystics, and dreamers, we do not in our present darkness speak face-to-face with the Sun/Son. Nicodemus was blessed indeed. But everyone, even Peter and Nicodemus, meets Jesus through the inevitably challenging combination of their bodies, personal histories, institutional histories, times, personalities, fears, hopes, likes, dislikes—and the aid of the Holy Spirit.

Even Peter, one of the people who knew Jesus best, believed in a Christ who would overthrow Rome to great glory and bring the Jewish people back to dominion over Israel. Like Peter, we all have our own ideas about who Jesus is, ideas mired in our cultural expectations of saviorship. With varying degrees of self-awareness, each one of us may worship self-help Jesus, historical Jesus, super-angry Jesus, archconservative Jesus, lefty anarchist Jesus, or some combination thereof. Sometimes these caricatures capture aspects of Jesus well, but they exaggerate some features while diminishing others. Sometimes they distort him beyond recognition. The church has witnessed the disastrous social consequences of some of these representations: Jesuses in the Middle Ages who encouraged murdering the Jews, Jesuses during the American Civil War who were pro–chattel slavery, and Jesuses who support capital punishment today. How are we to avoid these pitfalls in our ideas about Jesus and his character?

C. S. Lewis offered a persuasive answer. In his preface to Saint Athanasius's *On the Incarnation*, Lewis noted that wherever one finds Christian laity reading together, typically they are reading books by people of their own time and place, and usually of their own theological or ideological party. But as we seek truth, Lewis argued, the church's past writings are a gift to us. He wrote,

> Every age has its own outlook. It is specially good at seeing certain truths and specially liable to make certain mistakes. . . . Nothing strikes me more when I read the controversies of past ages than the fact that both sides were usually assuming without question a good deal which we should now absolutely deny. They thought they were as completely opposed as two sides could be, but in fact they were all the time secretly united—united with each other and against earlier and later ages—by a mass of common assumptions. . . . None of us can fully escape this blindness, but we shall certainly increase it, and weaken our guard against it, if we read only modern books. Where they are true they will give us truths which we half knew already. Where they are false they will aggravate the error with which we are already dangerously ill. The only palliative is to keep the clean sea breeze of the centuries blowing through our minds, and this can be done only by reading old books. Not, of course, that there is anything magic about the past. People were no cleverer then than they are now; they made as many mistakes as we. But not the *same* mistakes. They will not flatter us in the errors we are already committing; and their own errors, being now open and palpable, will not endanger us.[3]

Like Peter, recognizing Jesus's divinity and then almost immediately denying it because of his own ideas about what divinity

---

3. C. S. Lewis, preface to Saint Athanasius, *On the Incarnation*, ed. John Behr (Yonkers, NY: St. Vladimir's Seminary Press, 2011), 11.

should look like, we all read out of the context and history of the time in which we live. Our knowledge of the internet, chattel slavery, capitalism, the United States of America, T-shirts, the Holocaust, smartphones, and all the millions of things big and small that have happened over the last two thousand years doesn't disappear while we read. We swim in a sea of common assumptions and knowledge about science and the way the world works, what constitutes a human, right and wrong, and the things in between. Like fish, we can't escape, on our own, this ocean of unspoken commitments and beliefs.

More specifically, we read out of our own bodies and places and life experiences. I inevitably read like a mother, trained scholar, and millennial American white woman. You may read differently. Though we are called to go back to the Gospels over and over, time and again our biases will cloud the text before us. It's hard to break out of this conundrum.

Lewis helps us here. The traditions and writings of the church of ages past are a gift. They keep, in Lewis's memorable phrase, "the clean sea breeze of the centuries blowing through our minds," clearing out the accumulated musty air behind the closed doors and windows of our own assumptions. In our reading, where we stumble and what we find meaningful both matter. Both reveal where we have culturally contained Jesus and expose our strengths and weaknesses in understanding him. As Lewis argued, the strangeness of the past illuminates the damaging things we believe in order to make Jesus more palatable, understandable, or like us.

This book explores the answers to Jesus' question "Who do you say I am?" from medieval artists, mystics, and theologians. Some of these answers are metaphorical; some are drawn directly from Scripture. They do not wholesale replace our own answers to the question but enrich and sometimes even correct them. In reading these exploring, adoring, faithful witnesses from the past, we can come to know Jesus—and ourselves— better. What we find strange or beautiful in these medieval witnesses can reveal our concerns, hidden biases, and even new truths. They also teach us new and profound ways to love him. As such, this book is not meant to be read as a straightforward work of medieval history or theology or literary criticism. It is instead a conversation with literature, history, and theology, an interpretive process—a wrestling with the medieval church on that tricky question from Jesus. None of the medieval representations in these chapters can capture Christ in his fullness, yet each uniquely highlights aspects of his character through art, metaphor, and style. I like to think of them as different faces of Jesus.

Here you will meet a Jesus who wears armor, slays dragons, and jousts in tournaments for the souls of sinners. You will meet a Jesus who lactates and breastfeeds his beloved babies, who gestates them in his wounds on the cross and gives birth in the agony of his death. You will meet the frightening yet winsome Jesus enthroned on doomsday, who looks in the eyes of every person who ever lived. You will meet a Jesus who is the passionate, sensual lover of your soul. You will meet a Jesus who is a good medieval domesticized Christian who receives his saintly mother's cooking from angels in a sort of divine take-out delivery service. You will meet the abstract Jesus of the University, who is described with a specialized and precise vocabulary that has much to offer us today. And you will meet again—because we have all met him before, though not necessarily on these terms—the suffering Jesus on the cross, whose every drop of blood speaks grace and mercy and love to *you specifically*.

Why Medieval?

Why explore medieval poetry and theology, in contrast to return-ing to the early church, the Reformation, or another familiar time period? Those readings would help us too. But the medieval period and its writings, thought, and art are especially foreign to most of us—and they're weird and fun. Naturally, as a medievalist, I am a little biased. But medieval texts have again and again led me to Jesus and to the expectations I have read onto him.

In graduate school, I attended a class that was reading Geoffrey Chaucer's *Canterbury Tales*, perhaps the most famous English medieval poem. Specifically, we were reading "The Parson's Tale," a long, dry moral treatise on the seven deadly sins. Chaucer's fictional Parson has just spent lines and lines discussing "sin in clothing" as a sign of the mortal sin of pride. His favorite target: short-cut jackets that highlighted the extremely tight and reveal-ing hose many courtly men wore toward the end of the fourteenth century. Imagine reading this passage aloud with a group of adults stifling giggles as they attempt to appear intelligent and scholarly:

> Alas, some of them show their bulge, and the wrapping of their hose makes the horrible swollen members look like they have the malady of a hernia. Their buttocks look like the hind part of a she-ape during a full moon. Moreover, their wretched, swollen members, that they show through multi-colored hose, one side white and one side red, make it seem as though half their shameful private parts were on fire. . . . Their buttocks are full horrible to gaze upon.[4]

---

4. Geoffrey Chaucer, "The Parson's Tale" in *The Riverside Chaucer*, ed. Larry D. Benson, 3rd ed. (Boston: Houghton Mifflin, 1987), ll. 423–27. Lightly translated by myself for easier reading.

The Parson ends this colorful meditation with a negative comparison of these flashy, immodest dressers to the "honestitee," the propriety or decorum, of Jesus and his disciples: "that foul part [the aforementioned horrible buttocks] they show to the people proudly in spite of propriety, the propriety that Jesus Christ and his friends were observed to show in their lives."[5]

Full horrible buttocks! This passage would never leave anyone's memory. (You're welcome.) But surprisingly, the Parson's hilarious critique of medieval men's fashion is not what I recall most about reading this tale together in class. Upon reading the Parson's prim commentary on the decorum of Jesus and his disciples, my professor exclaimed, "I never met a Jesus like that! What Jesus is he talking about? I've never read anything in the Gospels about Jesus's modest taste in clothes." This comment initially baffled me. In all this unforgettable sequence, why would you focus on this aside about modest Jesus and his friends?

I had not even noticed the strange Jesus my professor pointed out. I was well acquainted with a version of Jesus that *did* care what people—or at least girls and women—wore. I came of age in the 1990s and early 2000s, around the height of promise rings and purity culture. As a young woman, I measured the hems of my shorts with my fingertips many times to make sure they weren't too short. I went swimming with a tank top on over my bikini so as not to thoughtlessly tempt my brothers in Christ. To me, the truly strange part about Chaucer's Jesus was that he focused on *men's* modesty, not that he cared about clothes.

I began to notice that my experiences as a woman growing up at the tail end of the twentieth century in the American evangelical church affected my ideas of Jesus more than I realized.

My professor would never have experienced those same social pressures. I had read those expectations back onto Jesus, who never discussed personal modesty in the Gospels. I had read the New Testament on my own and in church many times by this point in my life. Yet it took a literature professor and a six-hundred-year-old text condemning sexy jackets for me to realize I had superimposed my assumptions and culture onto Jesus.

Beyond the bizarre moment given by the Parson, I listened to and learned from lovers of Christ like William Langland, Julian of Norwich, Saint Bernard of Clairvaux, Pope Gregory the Great, and Margery Kempe. These medieval voices gave me new perspective. They highlighted aspects of Jesus I had overlooked. They revealed characteristics I had ascribed to Jesus without thinking much about it at all.

Our lack of cultural familiarity or personal comfort with medieval ideas makes these writings ideal for discovering aspects of Jesus's character that may be hiding in plain sight. The absurdity of passages like Chaucer's and the beauty, even shock, of passages from writers like Julian of Norwich or William Langland emphasize ideas otherwise easily missed.

We are less familiar as a society with the European Middle Ages than the period of the early church or, on its other end, the Protestant Reformation and Catholic Counter-Reformation and all that followed.[6] The European medieval period, meaning approximately 500 to 1500 AD, has a generally poor reputation. Some of it used to be called "the Dark Ages." The time period after the medieval is traditionally called the Renaissance, meaning "rebirth." Eighteenth- and nineteenth-century historians divided the

---

6. If you are unfamiliar with the era and its beliefs, Eamon Duffy's *The Stripping of the Altars*, 2nd ed. (New Haven: Yale University Press, 2005) is a wonderful place to begin.

Renaissance clearly from the medieval, seeing its new theology, new science, and new art as vast improvements in the European world. The modern colloquial phrase "to get medieval" means to become particularly violent. People typically use "medieval" as a synonym for something hopelessly outdated, vulgar, filthy, or inhumane.

In Protestant Christianity, the reputation of the Middle Ages is decidedly negative. Corruption and superstition characterized that period of the church. "Indulgences," some Protestants mutter, prompted by the sometimes righteous, sometimes erring wrath of Martin Luther and John Calvin. If you're Roman Catholic, you may have the opposite issue when reading medieval texts. To you, the medieval era may evoke a time of social and religious harmony before the fragmentation of the Reformation. Some Catholics harbor a romantic nostalgia toward the medieval era. Nostalgia can limit an honest reading of these texts almost as much as Protestant negativity because both attitudes thrive on the assumption that one has already mastered what it meant to be a person living in the medieval era. In reality, however, the medieval era is much bigger and stranger than the confines of either comfortable judgment or comfortable nostalgia.

I began reading medieval texts because, to my joyful surprise, I learned that *medieval Christians loved Jesus.* They wrote about Jesus incessantly, compulsively, athirst with love, devotion, and creativity. They possessed vast Christian imaginations, often more expansive and interesting than many of the Christians who preceded or followed them. I discovered that writers of this period were far more comfortable than we today in thinking about Jesus metaphorically, highlighting particular and peculiar attributes, and crafting new stories about him. Their narrative freedom, delight in allegory and metaphor as paths to truth, and cultural difference offer us the gift of strange new insights—the gift of surprise.

The Discipline of Openness: Approaching Old Books

Everyone—liberal or conservative or something else entirely, any gender, age, or race—will be surprised by what they encounter if they seriously attend to a book written seven hundred years ago. Present-day dichotomies no longer neatly apply. We may be shocked to find out that we have painstakingly constructed histories to fit our ideologies, histories that would have seemed strange to the people living within them. These moments of shock and surprise are gifts. We need this gift of surprise more than ever today, living as we do in a highly polarized culture. Surprise can break one out of preconceived notions about the way the world works, about the way God works, about the way people work.

Such surprise is like a hike. You thought one path was the only route to your desired location, the vista at the top of the mountain. You have taken that path many times and know every step and every viewpoint. It's a popular hike, and you see the same folks regularly walking it with you. Suddenly, you stumble upon a way nearly forgotten, an old, overgrown, winding footpath. You've passed it before, but this time you decide to take it and see what happens. To traverse this way, sometimes you trip over large roots and clamber over craggy rocks. It's intimidating because you have not gone this way before. Once you learn how to stay on your feet and can look up from the uneven ground, you discover something. You're on the same mountain, but it has totally different views of the surrounding mountains and plains and diverse birds and beasts. You meet different people on this path than on your old hike. Some of them are a little odd. You realize you have a fuller understanding of the scenery, the wildlife living here, the whole mountain itself, than you ever had before.

The gift of surprise does not work wonders on its own. One can be surprised at something and then quickly dismiss it or forget about it. To transform a perspective, the gift of surprise requires the discipline of openness to the text before us. What do I mean when I use this odd combination of words, the discipline of openness?

First, reading requires discipline. When I use the word *discipline* in this context, I mean a deliberate practice, something that could also be called a *habit* once exercised enough. A discipline is cultivated, a form repeated over and over until it becomes ingrained and habitual, like beautiful calligraphy or the perfect free throw. It will be difficult or awkward at first, but eventually, a discipline can become a habit that comes easily and naturally.

A reader cultivates an attitude toward the book in front of her depending on what kind of book it is. With fiction, the reader wants to become thoroughly immersed in the novel's world. She lets her mind drift away into the story while losing her self-awareness and sometimes even her sense of time and place. I was particularly good at this extreme attention as a kid; it became a joke in my family that I temporarily lost my hearing while I read. If you've ever dreamily emerged from a novel and returned to your own body only to discover with dismay that it is three o'clock in the morning, you know this attitude well.

A textbook, on the other hand, requires different disciplines as the reader sharpens her awareness and memory recall, trying to absorb the information and file it away in her mind. Excellent students turn this discipline of information absorption into a habit or even a set of habits: one lights a candle, prepares a set of color-coordinated highlighters, and makes some coffee, signaling to the mind that serious learning is about to begin.

When I first started reading ancient works of literature and theology, I read suspiciously. I wanted these works to mirror back my understanding of truth, and I manipulated them so they would. I elevated the things I liked, things that felt like my kind of Christianity (a personal relationship with Jesus!). I side-eyed and avoided the things I found questionable (the overwhelming medieval interest in suffering, ugh). I measured these diverse writers against an invisible standard of truth—my vision of "good" Christianity as I had understood it in that period of my life. I was reading out of my own time and place with well-armed guards instructed not to let anything suspiciously heterodox pass the gates of my belief into my head and heart. *Surprise!* As an American raised in the evangelical church, I encountered a lot of things in medieval writing that did not look like my faith. But as I read more and more of my medieval brothers and sisters and learned to practice the discipline of openness, I came to recognize some of my strange, culturally contingent beliefs and the richness these long-dead people offered to me freely and charitably.

One can read suspiciously in any direction on the political and theological spectrums of belief. When you read these medieval works today, it does not matter whether you are evangelical, Unitarian, Roman Catholic, or atheist. Medieval writers will challenge everyone who picks up their texts. Feminists, myself included, will wince: all medieval writers are misogynistic, even women. Some actively hated women, while others were simply infected by their culture, which consistently devalued women. One response then may be to cast them all into the fire. Some more theologically conservative folks will be disturbed that a group of medieval theologians preached something close to a theology of universalism—toss them into the dustbin of history! However, if unchecked, this process will inevitably lead to one outcome. You will be left with only your own guts for your guide (and maybe some of your most sycophantic friends) because you agree on all issues with only yourself. These gut instincts and feelings are important and worth devoted attention, but sometimes we need more. Though I know my body intimately, I need doctors to help me when I'm sick because they have a perspective and body of knowledge I do not possess. We need the works of the past to help us see beyond our own time-bound limitations.

Sometimes discernment requires suspicion. Gullible reading wreaks as much havoc, or more, as an overly suspicious mode (a fact we know too well today, in the age of Facebook and YouTube). Suspicion often leads us to truth. But suspicious reading, especially antagonistic suspicious reading, has its limits when it becomes the primary, first response to foreign ideas. When we read books from other times and cultures, we must deliberately practice an initial openness while we read. Treasure your surprise. Note the places in the text you trip over in discomfort, shock, or plain confusion. Of course, this openness does not mean you should embrace all medieval lessons. I would prefer we did not return to burning heretics at the stake. But practicing the discipline of openness means learning to listen quietly and wait deliberately before making judgments, to practice humility. This humble discipline entails acknowledging that you, as the twenty-first-century reader, are not in possession of all the answers and may need guidance or correction. Then processes of discernment can be welcomed back after that initial openness and serious attention.

Learning to Read like a Child

How can we read humbly? The fourteenth-century contemplative theologian and first documented woman writer in English, Julian of Norwich, can help us understand. In 1373, during a life-threatening illness, Julian experienced a series of what she called "showings": sounds, sights, and words given to her by God. One of her very first showings concerned the Annunciation, the moment when Gabriel came to Mary to tell her she would bear a child. The Annunciation reveals what the reception of truth looks like in action:

> He brought our lady Saint Mary to my understanding. I saw her spiritually in bodily likeness, a simple and humble maiden, young, only a little older than a child, as she looked when she conceived. Also God showed me in part the wisdom and truth of her soul, wherein I understood the reverent beholding with which she beheld her God her creator, marveling with great reverence that he would be born of her who was a simple creature of his making. For this was her marveling: that he who was her maker would be born of her that was made. And this wisdom and truth, knowing the greatness of her maker and the created littleness of herself, made her say with great humility to Gabriel, "Behold me, God's handmaiden."[7]

Note how in Julian's portrait of the Annunciation, clusters of the same language appear over and over: beholding, reverent, maker,

7. *The Writings of Julian of Norwich: A Vision Showed to a Devout Woman and A Revelation of Love*, ed. Nicholas Watson and Jacqueline Jenkins (University Park, PA: Pennsylvania State University Press, 2006), 4.24–32. Throughout this book, I lightly translate all line citations from this edition for easier reading.

made, creature, creator, marveling. Julian's language emphasizes above all Mary's understanding of her own smallness in relation to the world and to God. The made would bear the Maker. Mary is young, little, simple, childlike, yet Mary's acknowledgment of her littleness helps her to receive the greatness that fashioned the universe with artful skill. Julian understood that Mary's profound wisdom sprang from this unabashed confession of her littleness. In her every interaction, she knew her bodily and spiritual limitations as a *creature*. Mary was fashioned and loved, which in turn allowed her to receive and love. Julian's description of her uses the language of birthing truth, of growing children, *of receiving and learning*.

With all these diminutive terms, Mary starts to sound like a child in her reception of divinity. Julian knew that children are the best at recognizing their own limitations. Some adults would rather die than admit their shameful need; children acknowledge their need without shame in the most humiliating and attention-drawing moments: on the toilet or loudly in the classroom, unembarrassed, even eager, to ask the same question over and over again. Children model learning in this way. Through the unashamed embrace of their limits, children learn invaluable skills like reading, controlling their bladders, and listening with patience.

There's an important reason this little, childlike Mary constituted one of Julian's first revelations. Mary showed Julian how to receive the confusing, occasionally frightening, always vast truth that emerged from her revelations. If we imitate children, our limitations become powerful sources of wisdom, like Mary at the Annunciation. We often ignore our particularities of time, place, and bodies and think of ourselves as limitless gods. But truthfully, we are much closer to children than gods. And as Mary and Julian knew, this childlikeness is not a curse but a profound gift. In the eighteenth chapter of Matthew, the disciples argue over who is the greatest in the kingdom of heaven—in other words, who is the most godlike. Jesus turns their expectations on their heads and proclaims, "Truly I tell you, unless you change and become like children, you will never enter the kingdom of heaven. Whoever becomes humble like this child is the greatest in the kingdom of heaven" (Matt. 18:3–4). Our embodiment is not something to be wished away, to be replaced with something coldly objective and omnipotent. The further one journeys into intimate knowledge of their created littleness and belovedness, the more possible becomes real communion with the past or with people who think differently than oneself. In our smallness lies the possibility of real connection and intimacy. We know this because Jesus Christ embraced the limitations of embodiment in his incarnation. He chose to share these childlike human weaknesses with us to form the kingdom of heaven. Julian saw, interpreted, and *learned to love* by imitating Mary.

When I am confronted with the disorienting and beautiful but terrifying vastness of Christ and his body here on earth, I may be tempted to stand my ground and hide in what *I* know. But openness to learning and confession of littleness can lead to new insight and practices of faith.

Reading old books in this humble mode creates space for actual community with these ancient witnesses of love. We are given the gift of dialogue with the past—a past saturated in beauty and love of Christ. We live in a perilous, often depressing world. So did the writers, artists, and theologians who portrayed these different versions of Jesus. These medieval faces of Jesus reveal human error, ingenuity, and often trust in a transformative charity. They remind us of Christ's love that binds us as the church, which suffuses and transcends history and cultures in surprising and unforeseen ways.

As we gaze at these medieval faces of Jesus, we learn to wait patiently, as a narrative or image may at first seem inaccessible or bizarre. We learn to listen, as we encounter beliefs wildly different from our own but that still profess love for the incarnate God. We learn to ask questions insistently and excitedly again, like a child. And like in any friendship, as we wait, listen, and question, we form community and learn other forms of loving well. Julian is my friend and my teacher. So are Thomas Aquinas and Bernard of Clairvaux, despite that they both would have disapproved of my teaching and study, created as I am in this female body. I listen to and learn from them as I do from my friends here in twenty-first-century America. I even love one of the more complex figures of this book, Nicholas Love. As my flawed brother, he has helped me better understand my urge to cram Jesus into a nice, manageable box.

I hope you too meet new friends and find beauty in these pages.

Chapter Two

The Judge

Beginning this book by exploring medieval depictions of Jesus as the Judge makes me feel a bit like the wandering preacher who would show up twice yearly at my undergraduate university campus. "Brother Ed" would plant himself in the "free speech corner" and apoplectically bellow mostly at female students about how the end of the world was coming.[1] When that final day arrived, Jesus would send them to hell posthaste because of their iniquitous lifestyle, mostly represented by their short shorts. Though we may not see short shorts the way "Brother Ed" did, we might share his conception of the Judge as a God of violent, personalized rage.

Around the same time, I encountered another grim version of the Judge when my English literature survey course read some sermons by Jonathan Edwards (1703–1758). The New England Puritan wrote his virtuosic, terrifying sermon, "Sinners in the Hands of an Angry God," to scare people into repentance. Some of the class, myself included, admitted to being unable to sleep after

---

1. Not his real name, which I do not know. I'm not sure if the "free speech corner" was a name I made up as an undergrad, a feature of all public land-grant universities, or just a funky thing at the University of Arizona. Either way, the speakers there were typically outrageous.

reading lines like this: "The God that holds you over the pit of hell, much as one holds a spider or some loathsome insect over the fire, abhors you, and is dreadfully provoked."[2] Fear your death and judgment; the only reason you're not in hell right now is because of Christ's divine whim. While listening to this sermon, Edwards's audiences screamed, wept, and converted by the hundreds.[3] What united Edwards with the less talented Brother Ed was a desperate compulsion to create a frisson of fright in their listeners to force them toward repentance. Christ as a stern, wrathful judge at the end of days has often led Christians to paralyzing terror—or worse, violence.[4]

I do not begin with Jesus as Judge to scare anyone into salvation. In fact, this chapter hardly considers hell or heaven at all. They are footnotes to the divine figure emanating power at the center of each artwork, play, or poem in this chapter. I begin with Jesus as Judge because of chronology: it's an older representation of Jesus that became somewhat eclipsed by Christ on the cross as the Middle Ages waxed and waned. But there's more to this image than its historical moment. In Jesus's role as Judge, we witness two inseparable facets of Christ's character: justice and mercy. Contra Brother Ed's ideas, wrath was not the central piece of the portrait of Jesus as Judge in the medieval era.[5] Of course, representations

2. Jonathan Edwards, "Sinners in the Hands of an Angry God" in *The Norton Anthology of American Literature: Shorter Sixth Edition*, ed. Nina Baym (New York: W. W. Norton, 2003), 213.

3. Harry Stout, "Edwards as Revivalist," in *The Cambridge Companion to Jonathan Edwards* (Cambridge: Cambridge University Press, 2007), 137–38.

4. From the medieval Joachimites to Anabaptists in the Münster Rebellion to more recently the Branch Davidians, traditions of apocalypticism—overwhelming focus that the end of days is imminent—often end in violence.

5. Broadly speaking, the Reformation focused more on God's wrath. See Pieter G. R. de Villiers, "'In Awe of the Mighty Deeds of God': The Fear of God in Early Christianity from the Perspective of Biblical Spirituality," in *Saving Fear in Christian Spirituality*,

of Jesus as Judge were still meant to provoke fear. Yet holy fear has nothing to do with loathing oneself, identifying as disgusting insects, or wearing short shorts. There is a fear rooted in wisdom, the wisdom of the body and of our own limitations. Jesus the Judge reminds us of our divine community and invites a fear that guides us to love our neighbor as we love ourselves.

Christ in Judgment

In the art of the early Middle Ages, Jesus was often represented as what is now called "Christ in Majesty"—whether that was as Lawgiver, King of Kings, *Pantocrator* (Ruler of the World), or the End-of-Days Judge. For many European cultures in the early Middle Ages, the divinity of Christ was more central to accounts and practices of faith in those years than his suffering humanity.[6] Christ the King was ruler of the universe, victor over sin and evil, represented through earthly ideas of imperial power and judgment. Triumph and kingly power even trickled into representations of the cross: artists often chose not to portray his pain.[7] In many eighth- and ninth-century crucifixes, Jesus was calm and august, even the cross revealing "his triumph over evil and

---

ed. Ann W. Astell (Notre Dame, IN: University of Notre Dame Press, 2020), and Ralph Keen, "The Reformation Recovery of the Wrath of God," in the same volume; David Aers discusses it in relation to election and predestination in *Versions of Election: From Langland and Aquinas to Calvin and Milton* (Notre Dame, IN: University of Notre Dame Press, 2020).

6. Rachel Fulton Brown, *From Judgment to Passion: Devotion to Christ and the Virgin Mary, 800–1200* (New York: Columbia University Press, 2002), pt. 1.

7. For more, see Jaroslav Pelikan, *The Illustrated Jesus through the Centuries* (New Haven: Yale University Press, 1997), ch. 8; Celia Chazelle, *The Crucified God in the Carolingian Era: Theology and Art of Christ's Passion* (Cambridge: Cambridge University Press, 2001).

revelation of cosmic majesty."[8] In some ivory gospel-book covers that depict the crucifixion, Jesus's body is ramrod straight as he gazes straight ahead with no indication of pain. Instead, we recognize his coming triumph and notice symbolic elements around him, like the defeated serpent at the foot of the cross.

Book-cover plaque with Christ on the cross, ivory, ca. 870–880, Walters Art Museum, Baltimore. (See the insert for larger and full-color versions of all images.)

Public Domain.

---

8. Chazelle, *Crucified God*, 9.

The tradition of imagery, iconography, of this regal lawgiver was consistent. Anonymous artists like the one who created the ninth-century Athelstan Psalter (see p. 24) drew upon scriptural imagery in the Hebrew prophets, the Gospels, Saint Paul's letters, and the Revelation of Saint John the Evangelist.[9] They were influenced by the majestic, awe-inspiring, gloriously beautiful Lord of Isaiah 6:1–3:

> I saw the Lord sitting on a throne, high and lofty, and the hem of his robe filled the temple. Seraphs were in attendance above him; each had six wings: with two they covered their faces, and with two they covered their feet, and with two they flew. And one called to another and said,

> "Holy, holy, holy is the LORD of hosts;
> the whole earth is full of his glory."

Artists began to combine inspiration from the majestic king in his throne room with the vision of the *parousia*, the second coming described by John of Patmos. Revelation 1:7 guided these artistic representations of Jesus the Judge:

> Look! He is coming with the clouds;
> every eye will see him,
> even those who pierced him,
> and all the tribes of the earth will wail on account
> of him.

So it is to be. Amen.

---

9. See Natalie Jones, "Ways of Seeing Christ the Judge: The Iconography of *Christ III* and Its Visual Context," *Neophilologus* 105 (2021): 261–77, https://link.springer.com/article/10.1007/s11061-021-09673-x.

John describes this end-of-days king as recognizably Jesus pierced and wounded, not God the Father. Christ the Judge descends from the clouds specifically to be seen by all the people. This is the final day of judgment, the end of the world as we know it, and the time when graves will open up for bodies and souls to rejoin and either reign in blessedness or suffer in the lake of fire.

Christ in Majesty, Athelstan Psalter, manuscript illumination, ca. 9th century, Cotton MS Galba A.XVIII fol. 2v, British Library, London.

Public Domain.

Doom Paintings:
Meeting Jesus the Judge

In the late Middle Ages, the idea of judgment day was ubiquitous, painted on the walls of countless parish churches in England and on the Continent. Ominously, these paintings were called Doom paintings, or simply Dooms. We associate doom with dramatic movie villains—"Prepare to meet your doom!"—or perhaps the nuclear doomsday clock, counting down humanity's precious seconds to nuclear annihilation. Doom, however, is simply related to the ancient word *deem*, which we still use today, meaning "to judge."

Doom paintings were usually the largest in the church.[10] As a medieval parishioner, you would have gazed at the massive Christ the Judge after or even as you listened to the priest's homily and watched him raise up the body of Christ. In a culture where literacy wasn't as universal as it is today, such pictures, alongside sermons, plays, and storytelling, made up a huge part of an ordinary layperson's scriptural teaching.[11] We glimpse a world where the idea of Jesus as the end-of-days judge—and oneself either singing peacefully with angels or prodded by devils toward a yawning hellmouth—loomed large in the collective imagination.

The second coming of Christ was painted according to the same formula from about 1100 to 1500.[12] In every Doom, Jesus

---

10. Roger Rosewell, *Medieval Wall Paintings* (Oxford: Shire, 2014), 41.

11. Pope Gregory the Great famously wrote in a letter to Serenus, "What writing (*scriptura*) does for the literate, a picture does for the illiterate looking at it, because the ignorant see in it what they ought to do; those who do not know letters read in it. Thus, especially for the nations (*gentibus*), a picture takes the place of reading." *S. Gregori Magni registrum epistularum libri VIII–XIV*, ed. D. Norberg (Turnhout: Brepols, 1982), XI, 10, pp. 873–76, trans. L. G. Duggan in "Was Art Really the 'Book of the Illiterate'?," *Word and Image* 5 (1989): 227–51, https://doi.org/10.1080/02666286.1989.10435406.

12. Rosewell, *Wall Paintings*, 41.

sits in authority, towering over the multitude gathered beneath him. On an arch at the parish church of St. Thomas in Salisbury, England, painted around 1470, Jesus sits upon a rainbow, with his feet on a smaller rainbow. The rainbows remind us that he fulfills all his promises. A red cloak is draped around his shoulders and knees, with his chest bare and hands extended to clearly show the wounds of his passion. On his right is Mother Mary, to his left John the Evangelist. Angels hover around him, some holding the instruments of the crucifixion. Below Christ sit the twelve disciples.

The Doom Painting at St. Thomas, plaster wall painting,
ca. 1470–1500, Salisbury, Wiltshire, UK.

Further below, the action of doomsday crackles. On the left, naked bodies emerge from the ground, helped out by angels. They are the dead, rising from their burial sites to join Jesus in heaven. On the right also, the dead come forth. Yet devils are herding them into the mouth of hell. Despite their nudity, many figures on both sides curiously wear hats. Crowns, floppy farmer hats, miters, and papal tiaras perch incongruously atop naked bodies rejoicing with the angels or wailing in the fire of hell. The hats reveal that damnation is equal opportunity: king, pope, and peasant alike must account for their choices.

This picture of damnation as equal opportunity is a word of comfort along with fear. As a medieval peasant may have felt under the yoke of feudalism, I often feel like I live at the whims or inaction of inept or corrupt government, billionaires, lobbyists, big tech, and other overwhelmingly powerful forces in the world. In the last seven days of writing this chapter, there's been ample evidence of evil. In Buffalo, New York, a white shooter went looking for Black people to kill and slaughtered them while they were grocery shopping. In Uvalde, Texas, a teenage gunman killed nineteen children, beautiful images of God; meanwhile, politicians publicly fretted over preserving access to the lethal weapons used to killed them. One of the largest American Protestant denominations was revealed to have consistently covered up abuse and lied to its people.[13] Earthly powers like white supremacy, callous government officials, and power-hungry pastors devour small ones in their path. Yet in the Doom, the symbols of utmost worldly power congregate below Christ. Kings, popes, and cardinals, naked except for their

---

13. Robert Downen, interviewed by Terry Gross, "How the Southern Baptist Convention Covered Up Its Abuse Scandal," *Fresh Air* on NPR, June 2, 2022, https://www.npr.org/2022/06/02/1102621352/how-the-southern-baptist-convention-covered-up-its-widespread-sexual-abuse-scand.

hats, come face-to-face with someone on a different plane of being than themselves to whom they are held accountable. The promise of answering unanswered evil, acknowledging the recognized and unrecognized wrongs of the mortal world—*everlasting justice and compassion*—is ultimately what Christ the Judge signifies.

It's a promise, a prophecy, and a call for action now. *Thy kingdom come, thy will be done, on earth as it is in heaven*, as we pray every Sunday. We cannot just point fingers at tyrants, billionaires, and pundits. Those hats remind us that *we* are there too—us and the medieval folks, the whole of humanity. It is the end of the age, and all the bodies have come forth from their graves or the ocean or the dust to account. Unlike, say, the crucifixion, portrayals of Jesus the Judge include you as a participant in history's denouement.

A poem in Old English, now called *Christ III*, expands Revelation 1:7 into a thrilling passage of poetry. Likely composed in the tenth century, this poem appears in the Exeter Book, the largest known collection of Old English poetry, including a bunch of riddles (one inspiration for Gollum and Bilbo's riddles in *The Hobbit*). Old English is incomprehensible to English speakers today. If you were to look at the Exeter Book, you wouldn't be able to read it at all![14] Old English was the forebear of English that was written and spoken before the Norman invasion of 1066; it does not include the influx of vocabulary from French and Latin into English that emerged over centuries from that event.

The anonymous poet of *Christ III* had a haunting title for Jesus the Judge: *Medor*, "the Measurer."[15] The Measurer sits in

---

14. You can view the Exeter Book online at https://www.bl.uk/collection-items/exeter-book.

15. *Christ III*, trans. Aaron K. Hotstetter, *Old English Poetry Project*, l. 876, accessed July 2022, https://oldenglishpoetry.camden.rutgers.edu/christ-iii/. The entirety of *Christ III* is available in a free translation online with the Old English Poetry Project by Rutgers University.

judgment as humankind comes before him. In another evocative phrase from the poem, humans "bear their breast-hoard before the Child of God."[16] In other words, each body comes before the Measurer bearing all their tender, bitter, miserable, precious secrets to lay before him. Every unloving word, every knife-edged thought, every true gift of love and attention emerges from the "breast-hoard" of each person and comes to the light. They unfold like fabric for the shears; they tumble like wheat before the scythe.

Jesus the just judge calls us to remember that our actions—our individual, random, intentional, loving, stupid, cruel, bland actions, conversations, and thoughts—have consequences. The Doom is a mirror, reflecting to us the choices we have made in community. From their place at the center of human life, in the parish church, one of the few places where rich and poor come together, Doom paintings depict two kinds of relationships: the lateral relationships between humankind and the vertical relationship between Jesus and each individual soul. Jesus the Judge is not meant to make us focus on one moment at the consummation of history. Rather, he directs our attention toward life in human community *right now*.

Justice and Judgment

When we think about justice, or the lack thereof, we might consider courts of law or governing bodies. Of course, these should be places of justice. However, as medieval people knew, justice is not primarily abstract nor extended only through law. *Justice is always relational*; it occurs in relationship, between people. And justice is a practice. The great medieval theologian Thomas Aquinas

---

16. *Christ III*, l. 1072.

defined justice as "a habit, whereby a person renders to each one his or her due by a constant and perpetual will."[17] The flexibility of this definition allows us to ponder how one person's due might be different from another person's, given their personal and institutional history. Justice is not one-size-fits-all. Context matters.

At times, the practice of justice will be personal, occurring in conversations face-to-face, in carefully chosen and respectful language, in acts of solidarity and presence. In other moments, the practice of justice will be more impersonal, via voting booths or financial support. Yet it will always be relational, determined by the needs of our communities large and small. Doom paintings were deliberately placed inside each parish church, at the heart of relationship, celebration, lamentation, and community in every village and town. When faced with Jesus on his rainbow throne, we must learn to ask how each of us can render to the other person their due, as a fellow beloved child of God.

Another representation of Jesus the Judge gives us a vivid understanding of this idea. Medieval mystery plays depicted stories from Scripture in a series, sometimes all the way from Genesis to Revelation. These were not performed by professional actors but by members of guilds like carpenters, shipbuilders, or goldsmiths. These plays brought liturgy to life; biblical history unfolded in your time and place, enacted by and through your neighbors' bodies. The doomsday play put on by the mercers (merchants) at York was impressive. They had equipment to lower Jesus, a masked member of their guild, on a "rainbow timber."[18]

---

17. Thomas Aquinas, *Summa Theologiae*, trans. Laurence Shapcote, ed. John Mortensen and Enrique Alarcon (Lander, WY: Aquinas Institute for the Study of Sacred Doctrine, 2012), II-II.58.1.

18. *The York Corpus Christi Plays*, ed. Clifford Davidson (Kalamazoo, MI: Medieval Institute, 2011), 499.

Angels—both puppets and actors—surrounded him, and they held the instruments of the passion. It would have looked like the top part of a doomsday painting come to life. The blessed and damned flocked below him.

In an adaptation of Revelation and Matthew 25, some of the blessed come before Christ, and he thanks them for having fed him when he was hungry, clothed him when he was naked, and cared for him when he was sick. The confused folks ask in wonder, "When did we feed you, Lord? When did we do these deeds?" Christ answers,

> My blessed children . . .
> > When any had need, night or day,
> > Asked your help, they had it soon.
> > Your free hearts never said nay . . .
> > But as often times as they would pray,
> > They needed but to endure and request their boon.[19]

It's a powerful idea, the church as an answer to prayers of the needy. Christ is every person unclothed, in prison, oppressed, or ill, and the church's answers to them are the church's answers to Jesus.

The opposite is true as well. Christ tells the damned that they drove him out with blows, that they closed their ears and eyes to his suffering, that they refused to visit him because he was poor, imprisoned, or despised. The damned cry out in horror, "When did we show you this unkindness?"[20] And Jesus replies,

---

19. "Doomsday," *York*, 309–16. All quotes translated into modern English by myself.
20. "Doomsday," *York*, 353–54.

"As often as it happened,
That needy asked anything in my name,
You heard them not, you covered your ears,
Your help to them was unavailable [*no3ht at hame,*
literally, not at home].[21]

Again, Christ aligns himself with the poor, imprisoned, sick, and suffering. We literally send Jesus away—our help is not at home—when we close our minds and eyes to the afflicted.

The Old English poem *Christ III* describes the people who fall into hell as "mind-blinded men, / harder than flints" (l. 1187). Justice calls for us to reject the temptation to harden ourselves into stony, flintlike people, unheeding of the needs of others. Jesus the Judge asks us to consider, Am I mind-blinded by my upbringing, my personal commitments, or my choices? Have I built a careful intellectual defense system that hardens my heart against people I disagree with or do not like, who are actually Jesus in disguise? Aquinas explains why he adds "constant and perpetual will" into his definition of justice: humans are often willing to render justice to one person but not another, or in regard to one particular issue but not the next. Today we see our sad inconstancy on both public and personal levels: political parties loudly proclaim their "protection" of one particular kind of life while ignoring or demeaning the next (migrants, prisoners, people of color, LGBTQ+, unborn children, women, those with mental illness, the list goes on). People reflect this lack of care and inconstancy in personal relationships too. True justice unfailingly commits to each person's humanity, recognizing the Christ in each one.

---

21. "Doomsday," *York*, 357–60.

Fear as Gift

When you look at the Doom or imagine the York doomsday play, are you afraid or nervous? Medieval people were a lot more comfortable than we are with using fear to motivate, and these works of art are meant to evoke fear in those listening and looking. Fear as a teaching tool is complex, is usually misused, and often goes wrong. The historian Rachel Fulton Brown uses the example of Saint Peter Damian as someone haunted by the Jesus of judgment day. He repeatedly preached self-flagellation—flogging and physically punishing himself—to reduce his massive debt to God and make amends for his sins.[22] The specter of eternal damnation terrified him. He was weighed down by his own salvation and felt like he had to make amends, to live the best life possible, to merit eternal life. And even though modern people often associate medieval people with this kind of self-punishment, even at the time, some theologians criticized Peter Damian's choices.[23] I doubt that Jesus, the incarnate God who glorified the human body beyond any human expectations, desired poor Peter Damian's self-harm as a way to seek justice and cultivate proper fear.

Though he would disagree with me, holy fear is not Peter Damian's fear: an unending, deep-rooted anxiety that I'm never enough and can never do enough good to really be loved by God. Nor is it a moralistic fear of God that Pieter G. R. de Villiers described as "individual piety and an upright lifestyle" that can easily shrink into fear of hell and the upholding of norms.[24] No, holy fear is a wholesome fear that aids us to avoid becoming people of flint.

---

22. Brown, *Judgment*, 89–106.
23. Brown, *Judgment*, 98.
24. Villiers, "In Awe," 22.

So why use the baggage-laden word *fear* instead of *awe* or *respect*? The difference between awe or respect and fear is the difference between seeing the skeletons of dinosaurs at the Denver Museum of Nature and Science and witnessing a dinosaur in the flesh. A skeleton I would gape at, impressed that something so gigantic was once alive. Then I'd go about the rest of my day. But if I saw a live Tyrannosaurus rex, I would feel small down to my toes in the presence of its enormous power. Seeing the T. rex would determine my next action, my next thought. Perhaps I would tremble or hide or give thanks. I would keep a healthy distance from said dinosaur to avoid imitating *Jurassic Park*. This fear gives birth to humility, to the healthy recognition of my humanity and natural limitations.

It is healthy and reasonable for humans to be afraid of anything bigger or more powerful than we are. We *should* be cautious around large animals, venomous spiders, oceans, and dark places while surfing, skiing, or rock climbing. Small children must learn to be careful when jumping off furniture or walking by the edge of a pool. It would be bad for their formation if they did not learn this level of caution. Reasonable fear gives us the gift of remembering our limitations and practicing good judgment while enjoying a proximity to beauty, power, and the thrill of taking risks.

We fear Christ as we fear the ocean: for the staggering beauty and uncontrollable power. His incomprehensible justice and his perfect mercy overwhelm us. Scripture teaches that fear of God is the root of wisdom (Proverbs 1:7; 9:10). Even when Jesus was still on earth, he sometimes inspired fear. When Christ calmed the storm, he rebuked the disciples for their fear of the storm. And then their fear shifted and transformed as they recognized a power even greater than that of the storm: "He said to them, 'Why are you afraid? Have you still no faith?' And they were filled with great fear and said to one another, 'Who then is this, that even the wind and the sea obey him?'" (Mark 4:40–41). In Luke 7:11–17, when Jesus raises the son of a widow from the dead, the bystanders are lost in holy fear at the might of Christ's compassion.[25]

This holy fear extends to the church as the body of Christ with us on earth. Everyone else's presence in the Doom reminds us that we should also recognize the vast beauty and significance of each individual person, especially when we do not understand them. The paradox is that humans are often terrified of one another, yet not fearful enough of each other. We do not consider what we owe one another in our glory as images of God. In *The Weight of Glory*, C. S. Lewis writes,

> It is a serious thing to live in a society of possible gods and god-
> desses, to remember that the dullest most uninteresting person
> you can talk to may one day be a creature which, if you saw it
> now, you would be strongly tempted to worship, or else a hor-
> ror and a corruption such as you now meet, if at all, only in a
> nightmare. . . . It is in the light of these overwhelming possibil-
> ities, it is with the awe and the circumspection proper to them,
> that we should conduct all of our dealings with one another,
> all friendships, all loves, all play, all politics. There are no ordi-
> nary people. You have never talked to a mere mortal. Nations,
> cultures, arts, civilizations—these are mortal, and their life is
> to ours as the life of a gnat. But it is immortals whom we joke
> with, work with, marry, snub, and exploit.[26]

Given this dazzling immortality, given who we are made in the image of, it is a profound good to be wholesomely afraid of

---

25. See Villiers for a beautiful reading of this passage, "In Awe," 37–39.
26. C. S. Lewis, *The Weight of Glory* (New York: HarperCollins, 2001), 45–46.

violating another person's humanity. People who do evil, who cover up church abuse, who value material goods over fellow humans, who justify evil acts do not truly fear God or other images of God. How can even a flippant Twitter comment—let alone putting a person to death or not attending to pleas for racial justice—become acceptable or excusable in the flooding light of the knowledge of who we are and what we are becoming? Fear of Jesus the Judge becomes a gift for our practice of justice, in the radiant light of his justice. Such a fear softens flinty hearts.

The Doom paintings' presence at the heart of community in the parish churches prompts us to ask what we owe our neighbors in justice and mercy, our pale attempts at practicing the justice and mercy of the Judge. In *Tell It Slant*, Eugene Peterson examines the story of the good Samaritan. A religious scholar asks Jesus, "Teacher, what do I need to do to attain eternal life?" Jesus asks the scholar what God's law says about this question. The scholar answers rightly, that you love the Lord your God with all your heart, mind, and strength and that you love your neighbor as you love yourself. Jesus praises his answer. Then the scholar asks— perhaps, as Peterson notes, in an attempt to wriggle out of certain obligations—"Who is my neighbor?" Jesus tells the parable of the good Samaritan in response. Peterson writes about this answer:

> Jesus' story did not define the neighbor. It created a neighbor.
>
> Jesus' story puts a full stop for all time to all the variations on the question, "Who is my neighbor?" As Heinrich Greeven puts it, "One cannot define one's neighbor; one can only be a neighbor."[27]

---

27. Eugene Peterson, *Tell It Slant: A Conversation on the Language of Jesus in His Stories and Prayers* (Grand Rapids: Eerdmans, 2008), 42, quoting *Theological Dictionary*

"Am I a neighbor?" the Doom in the center of the neighborhood provokes the viewer to ask. "Am I seeing the immortal being, the image of God, Jesus himself, in every person I encounter?" prompt the doomsday plays. Neighborliness and fear of God are twinned. Saint Augustine of Hippo calls chaste fear of God a needle, while charity is the thread, stitching our lives together in the body.[28] To ask Christ for his judgment means to ask for the grace of becoming a neighbor.

Trembling in the Face of Compassion

This fear, transformed into humility, is different from being terrified by Christ the Judge. I still tend to edge around this vision of Jesus, but I had an epiphany the other day. In movies, either the villain or the hero often has a moment when they have to resort to stronger measures, to violence or cruelty, to save the day or get attention. If those movies or shows are poorly written, that person will announce, "No more Mr. Nice Guy!" I realized that I tend to think of Jesus the Judge as the divine version of "No more Mr. Nice Guy." I imagine him thinking something like this: "Getting humanity's attention on the cross did not work; the time has come for more brutal actions."

Yet something important about these later medieval portrayals of Jesus the Judge resists this interpretation: the prominence of his wounds. In most Dooms, Christ is only partially clothed.

of the New Testament, ed. Gerhard Friedrich, trans. Geoffrey W. Bromilley, vol. 6 (Grand Rapids: Eerdmans, 1968), 317.

28. See Augustine of Hippo, *Homilies on the First Epistle of John,* trans. Boniface Ramsey, in *Works of St. Augustine*, vol. I/14 (Hyde Park, NY: New City Press, 2008), 136; on this simile, read John Sehorn, "Threading the Needle: Fear of the Lord and the Incarnation in St. Augustine," in Astell, *Saving Fear,* 76–101.

As noted, in Salisbury, a red robe is draped over his shoulders and knees, but his torso remains exposed. In one of my favorite Dooms, by Fra Angelico (ca. 1425–1430), Jesus's white robe covers his whole body, but there's a gaping hole in it where his side wound appears (see insert, Fra Angelico, *Judgment Day*). *Christ the Savior and Judge* by Petrus Christus (ca. 1450) is not a traditional Doom, but on either side of Christ, slightly behind him, two angels linger, one holding a flowering branch of lilies, the other a sword. Each angel represents a facet of Christ's character as judge: He is justice. He is mercy. Neither Jesus's justice nor his mercy will be cheap; both have already cost him his life. He inevitably satisfies the demand of true justice, a justice beyond human capability. His justice is beyond a simple exchange of an eye for an eye, beyond even equality, which levels indiscriminately. The just and merciful God-man is front and center, dominating the picture. With one hand he cradles his side wound. The other is held open in wounded vulnerability at the consummation of history.

We are tempted to read these gestures as "look what you've done," a guilt-and-fear-inducing moment of horror at the violence of humanity, especially my own self-preserving violence of indifference and callous selfishness. This response is necessary and not without merit. For justice, there *must* be a reckoning with the realization, in the words of the Book of Common Prayer, that "We have left undone those things which we ought to have done; And we have done those things which we ought not to have done; And there is no health in us."[29] As Christians we are called to regularly speak words like these and mean them.

---

29. "Morning Prayer," *The Book of Common Prayer: The Texts of 1549, 1559, and 1662*, ed. Brian Cummings (Oxford: Oxford University Press, 2011), 241.

Petrus Christus, *Christ as the Man of Sorrows*, sometimes
called *Christ the Savior and Judge*, oil on panel, 1450,
Birmingham Museum, Birmingham, UK.

Photo by Birmingham Museums Trust, licensed under CC0.

At the same time, Christ's display of his wounds tells us, *I am
the same yesterday, today, and forever* (Heb. 13:8). It's not a "no
more Mr. Nice Guy" situation because he has not changed. Jesus
the Almighty Judge is the same Jesus who went willingly to the

cross, uncurling his fingers for the nails, refusing to defend himself against the violence of the world. His wounds preach his mercy to us, and that is why he displays them. In Petrus Christus's painting, we stand before the God who shares the power of his wounds in the face of our own wounds and the knowledge of how we have wounded others. Trembling in the presence of overwhelming compassion, we cannot help but be transformed. His mercy is as powerful and fear-inspiring as his justice; they are two parts of a perfect whole, embodied in his wounds.

The marriage of true justice and true mercy feels impossible, yet Christ's rainbow throne reminds us that he fulfills all promises. Julian of Norwich, the fourteenth-century contemplative, expressed our difficulty of believing in the combination of surpassing lovingkindness and power because frankly we have never seen that combination possible: "For some of us believe that God is almighty and can do all, and that he is all wisdom and knows all. But that he is all love and will do all, there we struggle."[30] Theoretically, we recognize God's strength and power to do everything, but it is hard for us to believe his love is so all-surpassing that he will do everything possible to love us—that he will indeed satisfy his promises of grace and love, everlasting justice and compassion. Judgment day is the fulfillment of God's character—that, in Julian's words, God is all love and will do all. The *parousia* is the promise yet to be accomplished. Lord Jesus the Judge, come quickly. Lord Jesus the Judge, make me a neighbor now.

30. *The Writings of Julian of Norwich: A Vision Showed to a Devout Woman and A Revelation of Love*, ed. Nicholas Watson and Jacqueline Jenkins (University Park: Pennsylvania State University Press, 2006), 73.24–25.

Meditation and Practices
Inspired by Jesus the Judge

Each chapter ends with Scripture, exercises, and a prayer. These are an invitation to meditate on some of the central ideas about Jesus. These are not necessary but truly invitational; practice them if you wish.

- Meditate on this segment from Psalm 51 (50 in the Latin Vulgate). If you like, read the psalm in its entirety. What stands out? What is difficult or encouraging?

> Have mercy on me, O God,
>> according to your steadfast love;
> according to your abundant mercy,
>> blot out my transgressions.
> Wash me thoroughly from my iniquity,
>> and cleanse me from my sin. . . .
>
> Hide your face from my sins,
>> and blot out all my iniquities.
>
> Create in me a clean heart, O God,
>> and put a new and right spirit within me.
> Do not cast me away from your presence,
>> and do not take your holy spirit from me.
> Restore to me the joy of your salvation,
>> and sustain in me a willing spirit. (vv. 1–2, 9–12)

- Listen to Gregorio Allegri's haunting Renaissance choral setting of this psalm, *Miserere mei, Deus*, available on most

streaming services. I like the version by the Tallis Scholars.
Keep the words of the psalm in your mind as you listen.
What image, thought, or feeling emerges during your quiet
listening?

- How can you be a neighbor to the people you encounter
  every day? Think of one simple practice that can build a
  habit of being a neighbor: learning the names of your actual
  neighbors and finding ways to serve them (shoveling snow,
  rolling trash cans to the curb, bringing cookies); calling a
  lonely relative to check in on them once a week; bringing a
  different struggling friend dinner each month; learning the
  name of and discovering how best to serve the person experiencing homelessness you see each day on your commute.
- The York doomsday Jesus invites us to make mercy "at
  home" in our bodies in the face of suffering and injustice. If
  possible, volunteer with an organization that combats injustice in your community, not just donating or praying from a
  distance (although I'm sure they would appreciate those as
  well). Some ideas might be organizations that provide food
  or housing for the impoverished, care for women and babies
  in need, help migrants and refugees, or support people of
  color through the work of antiracism.

Prayer

Pray Psalm 43, for yourself or for victims of oppression, to Jesus
the Judge:

> *Vindicate me, O God, and defend my cause [in other
> translations, often "Judge me"]*

against an ungodly people;
from those who are deceitful and unjust,
   deliver me!
For you are the God in whom I take refuge;
   why have you cast me off?
Why must I walk about mournfully
   because of the oppression of the enemy?

O send out your light and your truth;
   let them lead me;
let them bring me to your holy hill
   and to your dwelling.
Then I will go to the altar of God,
   to God my exceeding joy,
and I will praise you with the harp,
   O God, my God.

Why are you cast down, O my soul,
   and why are you disquieted within me?
Hope in God, for I shall again praise him,
   my help and my God.

Chapter Three

The Lover

Who wrote the following passage: a Harlequin novelist writing about a rakish duke seducing a lovely chambermaid, or a thirteenth-century German nun sworn to poverty and chastity writing about the incarnate God?

> And then he begins so to caress her that she becomes weak. She so begins to drink it all in that he becomes lovesick. Then he begins to limit the intensity, because he knows better her limits than she herself does.[1]

That's right, it's the nun. This sensual passage is only one of many from Mechthild of Magdeburg (ca. 1207–ca. 1282/1294). I was sitting in a coffee shop as I transcribed this passage, Mechthild's *The Flowing Light of the Godhead* open before me. I nervously peered around at the other coffee shop patrons, hoping they couldn't see my screen and assume I was about to write a racy boudoir scene.

---

1. Mechthild of Magdeburg, *The Flowing Light of the Godhead*, translated and introduced by Frank Tobin (New York: Paulist, 1998), 227.

The time has come for a rendezvous with Jesus our Lover.

Upon reading the word *lover*, you may feel less like Mechthild of Magdeburg and more like Liz Lemon in NBC's classic sitcom *30 Rock*: "Ooh, that word bums me out unless it's between the words 'meat' and 'pizza.'"[2] To speak of Jesus as a lover can feel either cheesy or creepy or somehow, horribly, both. The image can evoke the tacky synth of "Take My Breath Away" playing in the background of a sex scene. Or worse, it conjures the 1990s and early aughts purity culture inanity of teaching teenage girls that Jesus is their boyfriend until they get married, and then, well, they'll have a human husband they can finally sleep with. There have been other, even more toxic narratives about sexuality and Christianity, too many to list here, based on oppressive gendered expectations or the depersonalization of bodies that happens in a sex-saturated culture.

Perhaps the most painful obstacle impeding the idea of Christ as a lover is that in romantic or sexual relationships, many people have been used, abused, or unvalued as whole persons. When we think of Christ as our individual, personal lover, not just as the corporate, abstract lover of the church, the idea is often laden with the heavy and sometimes traumatic burdens—broken hearts, physical or sexual abuse, manipulation and cruelty—of our past human relationships.

At their best, medieval people are on to something in using this imagery. They portray the God-man who tenderly offers his body to us in the mutual submission of love. Christ's gentle homemaking in his death on the cross is the ultimate rejection

---

2. *30 Rock*, episode 2.8, "Secrets and Lies," directed by Michael Engler, written by Ron Weiner, featuring Tina Fey, Alec Baldwin, Jane Krakowski, and Tracy Jordan, aired December 6, 2007, on NBC.

of humanity's abusive power relations.[3] Encountering Christ through the language of embodied intimacy can help us to turn away from the frequent coercion or depersonalization of human sexual relationships and consider how we were made to desire and be desired—not exclusively in sexuality but as whole persons. Christ chooses each person in all their naked vulnerability. In his love, we taste delight, surrender our bodies and hearts, and become more like our Lover.

Sexy Bodies and Holy Language

Let us begin with the irony that almost all medieval thinkers believed virginity was superior to *any* form of sexual expression, inside or outside marriage. For medieval people, sex within marriage was acceptable, even pleasurable, but not exemplary. It was meant for human reproduction and to release what many saw as the weakness of sexual desire with as little sin as possible.[4] So it's rather odd to discover the enormous popularity of adopting the language of sex and bodies to portray the church's and each individual's relationship to Jesus! Women, men, celibate, married, envelope-pushing mystical writers and crusadingly orthodox abbots, sixth-century popes and fourteenth-century brewers' wives—they all found something compelling in the image of Jesus as our lover.[5]

---

3. Of course, not all medieval imagery of Christ as a lover does this—some of it simply replicates abusive power dynamics—but I have chosen passages that do.

4. This belief was widely held. For one such view, see Thomas Aquinas, *Summa Theologiae*, trans. Laurence Shapcote, ed. John Mortensen and Enrique Alarcon (Lander, WY: Aquinas Institute for the Study of Sacred Doctrine, 2012), *II.II.152.5.resp.*

5. Marriage to Jesus appeared over and over in medieval contemplative and devotional writing. A nonexhaustive list: Saint Bonaventure, Saint Bridget of Sweden, Saint Catherine of Siena, Henry Suso, Jan Ruusbroec, the Dominican preacher Johannes Tauler,

All this sexy language came from Scripture. Surprisingly, the biblical book Song of Songs was one of the most popular books of the Bible in the medieval church. Medieval Christians, especially monks, read it allegorically as a way of understanding Christ's love.[6] Gregory the Great, the influential theologian and pope from 590 to 604 AD, wrote about the Song of Songs and its capacities to awaken the soul. He neatly summed up the attitude of monastic writers toward this medieval bestseller:

> For allegory supplies the soul separated far from God with a kind of mechanism by which it is raised to God ... through means which are not alien to our way of understanding, that which is beyond our understanding can be known.
>
> Thus it is that in this book, called The Song of Songs, we find the words of a bodily love: so that the soul, its numbness caressed into warmth by familiar words, through the words of a lower love is excited to a higher. For in this book are described kisses, breasts, cheeks, limbs; and this holy language is not to be held in ridicule because of these words. Rather we are provoked to reflect on the mercy of God; for by his naming of the parts of the body by which he calls us to love we must be aware of how wonderfully and mercifully he works in us; for he goes so far as to use the language of our shameful loves in order to set our heart on fire with a holy love.[7]

Hadewijch, the Franciscan preacher David of Augsburg, Mechthild of Magdeburg, and a whole host of scraps and pieces from anonymous writers. A brief overview of the history of Jesus as bridegroom is in Jaroslav Pelikan, *The Illustrated Jesus through the Centuries* (New Haven: Yale University Press, 1997), ch. 10.

6. For more, see Ann Astell, *The Song of Songs in the Middle Ages* (Ithaca, NY: Cornell University Press, 1990).

7. Gregory the Great, "Exposition of the Song of Songs," excerpted in Denys Turner, *Eros and Allegory: Medieval Exegesis of the Song of Songs* (Kalamazoo, MI: Cistercian, 1995), 217–18.

Gregory's slightly begrudging point is that God mercifully and lovingly communicates to us in our current bodies and minds, using human lovemaking to bring us to the understanding and practice of holiness. He argues that the allegorical language of passionate love, even body parts, beckons us into a deeper, experiential understanding of God's love. The numb soul, worn down by sin and the cares and mundanity of embodied life, may be caressed into warmth. Jesus the Lover purposes to set us on fire with desire in our bodies and understandings, to woo with intimate vulnerability, to win returning love with his own ardent love.

Note that it is a man, and a celibate pope at that, who wrote about the value of this language. Today we still use Revelation- and prophet-inspired bride language for the church as a whole. We also sometimes describe Jesus as a spouse or lover for young virginal girls or professed women religious like nuns.[8] Sometimes the idea of Jesus as a lover gets oriented around gender and sexual experience—women in the place of the bride, men in the place of Christ the bridegroom. In contrast, medieval folks did not exclusively understand Jesus the Lover as a church-only or women-only metaphor. Jesus is the lover of each soul, all genders alike, a truth conveyed through bodily and marital themes and language.[9]

Medieval writers were ultimately considering Christ's desire in terms of the soul. Yet they realized that bodily language better conveys the power, intensity, and personality of desire than overly spiritualized language does. In English, "love" can be unhelpfully

---

8. The exclusive association of bride of Christ with a chaste girl or holy woman originates in "the religious debates of the sixteenth century," not any medieval or even patristic sources, per Rabia Gregory's thorough study, *Marrying Jesus in Medieval and Early Modern Northern Europe: Popular Culture and Religious Reform* (New York: Routledge, 2016).

9. See Gregory, *Marrying Jesus*, ch. 2; Henry Suso and Jan Ruusbroec are two prominent examples of medieval male brides of Jesus whose writings widely circulated.

broad. It can describe our feelings about a really good pair of socks or a soul mate. But to set a soul on fire, to cause hearts to leap with the joy of being fully known and fully longed for, Jesus the Lover speaks to us in the language of sensual love to foster our desire and to reveal his own. The scriptural allegory of embodied, erotic love becomes a dim mirror into which we can gaze to catch a glimpse of the infinitely greater, gleaming love of the incarnate God.

A Patient Lover

The vision of Christ as a lover took shape in a variety of writing, from mystical theological treatises to sermons to poetry. The suffering, knightly lover was a longstanding medieval theme, often appearing in tales of King Arthur and other swashbuckling tales of chivalry, where a faithful knight suffers deeply for his loyalty to a courtly lady because she is unfaithful, uninterested, or downright cruel.

One of my favorite medieval lyrics draws from the Song of Songs and these chivalric ideals to describe the love of Jesus. This fifteenth-century, untitled, anonymous poem begins "in the vale of restless mind" as the speaker of the poem seeks a "true-love."[10] Wandering the wilderness of his interior self, the speaker hears a voice and draws near, and the voice says this in "great dolor": "See, dear soul, my sides bleed, / *Quia amore langueo* [Because I swoon with love]."[11] A handsome man with a gracious face, covered with wounds from head to toe, sits under a tree. He introduces

---

10. Originally from Lambeth MS 853, in F. J. Furnivall, *Political, Religious, and Love Poems*, EETS, O.S. 15 (London, 1866), 180–88. Throughout, I call this *Quia amore langueo* and have lightly updated and translated it.

11. *Quia amore langueo*, ll. 1–3.

himself as "True-Love," never false, always in love with the soul. He describes his travails of showing his love to the soul in ways she can understand (the soul is usually referred to as "she," following the conventions of ancient languages like Latin and Greek, but it can refer to the soul of anyone). This anonymous poet marries the language of romance with the imagery of the crucifixion:

> I will abide til she be ready;
> I will to her send though she say nay;
> If she be reckless [without care] I will be ready,
> If she be dangerous [disdainful] I will her pray;
> If she do weep then bid I nay:
> My arms are spread to clasp her to.
> Cry once, "I come," now, soul, assay,
> > *Quia amore langueo.*[12]

These disparate things—brutal death and the gentle language of a patient lover—are united by the voluntary suffering of the lover for the beloved. In an echo of Christ's outstretched arms on the cross, the lover invites the soul into his embrace, but she rejects him. He will abide until she is ready to come. Love returned through force or fear is not perfect love. The true lover will wait in perfect patience and adoration as long as need be.

In another stanza that might strike us as curious, Christ's wounded side becomes the bridal chamber where rest, peace, and the consummation of love occur:

> In my side I have made her nest.
> Look in, how wide a wound is here:

---

12. *Quia amore langueo*, ll. 65–72.

> This is her chamber, here shall she rest,
> That she and I might sleep together.
> Here she may wash if any filth were;
> Here is succour for all her woe.
> Come if she will, she shall have cheer,
>   *Quia amore langueo.*[13]

Christ's wounds were central to medieval devotion, especially his side wound. Similar to the modern-day Roman Catholic devotion of the Sacred Heart, Christ's wounded side was venerated and glorified as the passage to his inner heart. Often illustrated in prayer books, the side wound demonstrated his comfort to the weary and suffering—a path into love that welcomes, cleanses, and shelters the soul. Jesus offers a home of love. The beloved twentieth-century writer Henri Nouwen wrote on John 15:4, "When Jesus says: 'Make your home in me as I make mine in you,' he offers us an intimate place that we can truly call 'home.'"[14] A weary body comes home to a hot shower, to a comforting friend in the midst of mourning, to sleep after a horrible day.

Some medieval theologians, poets, and artists explore the imagery of the side wound in ways that may surprise a present-day reader, drawing out the abundant fruitfulness and beauty of Christ's love in our lives. In a manuscript now at Princeton University, flowers spring out of Christ's bleeding heart. "Well of lyfe," reads the image. The side-wound themes and imagery invert the traditional roles of Christ as bridegroom and the Soul as bride by portraying Jesus as the one who is inviting his beloved into his body. Christ's side wound was often drawn shaped like a

---

13. *Quia amore langueo,* ll. 57–64.
14. Henri Nouwen, *Lifesigns: Intimacy, Fecundity, and Ecstasy in Christian Perspective* (New York: Image, 2003), 14.

vulva. Inspired by the yearning lover of the Song of Songs, many medieval writers and artists saw theological importance in Christ's taking on the traditionally feminine role of being pierced with love. This parallel is no accident. It's not even a Freudian slip. In some illustrations, Christ even gives birth from his side wound. He is the mother of the church, his wounds the womb through which we are born again. As our lover, he is profoundly fruitful. He forms us in blooming beauty through his tender desire.

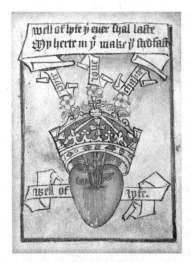

Wounded Heart of Christ as the "Well of Lyfe," manuscript illumination, ca.1500, MS Taylor 17, fol. 10v, Princeton University Library, Princeton.

Public Domain.

Christ's Side Wound, attributed to Jean Le Noir, The Prayer Book of Bonne of Luxembourg, Duchess of Normandy, manuscript illumination, before 1349, fol. 331r, Cloisters Collection, Metropolitan Museum of Art, New York.

Public Domain.

Does this tradition of imagery startle you? Modern readers often project cultural discomfort around sex and gender backward onto historical people and ideas. It's important to pay attention to the places in these ancient texts and images that cause discomfort or confusion, as they are often places that helpfully challenge our assumptions today of who God is or what Christianity should look like. Medieval people do not follow contemporary norms. Such illustrations were not meant to be titillating. The makers using feminine anatomy to portray Christ's side wound desired to emphasize facets of his character as a lover. As God, Jesus transcends traditional masculine or feminine cultural ideals. He encapsulates the best of all lovers, for all are made in his image. He submits, he waits in patience without anger, he invites us to enter into him. He is a vulnerable lover whose love is more capacious, generous, and fruitful than that of any human spouse.

My favorite stanza of the poem, more adaptation from the Song of Songs, reflects on this abundant, homey fruitfulness of his passionate love:[15]

> My sweet spouse, let us to play—
> Apples been ripe in my garden;
> I shall thee clothe in new array [clothes],
> Thy meat [food] shall be milk, honey, and wine.
> Now, dear soul, let us go dine—
> Thy sustenance is in my bag, lo!
> Tarry not now, fair spouse mine,
>   *Quia amore langueo.*[16]

This Jesus is playful, gentle, and generous. Even more, he is making a home for us. Frederick Dale Bruner, in his commentary on "abide in me" (John 15:4), calls Jesus "our homemaker."

---

15. Song of Songs 2:4–5; 4:16; 8:5.
16. *Quia amore langueo*, ll. 81–88.

"Make your home in this special love of mine (and relax)," translates Bruner. [17]

We are back in Eden, but it is Eden healed and transformed. We have been beckoned into the home that Christ has created with his body, where wine, a feast, and fresh, beautiful clothes await us after our long journey home. Christ has turned the illicit pleasures of Adam and Eve into a bridal feast of joy. The apples are ripe and ready. Invited to eat the fruit, we savor the almost unbearable sweetness and newfound knowledge of how much we are desired and valued. The intimacy of the table welcomes us. Our Lover invites us to fruitful, gentle, slow-growing love that welcomes, heals, and nourishes his beloved.

The Naked Soul Meets Her Lover

Poetic language, as in *Quia amore langueo*, is one thing. But as we meet medieval people like Mechthild, Margery Kempe, or Henry Suso, we realize that some medieval people wrote seriously about experiencing, in different ways, actual marriage to the Godhead. Male and female, priests and laypeople, they wrote about their own bodily and spiritual ecstasy in meeting Christ in visions and bodily experiences, in divine union that uses language inspired by marriage ceremonies and sex. More surprisingly, such experiences were not seen as confined to the otherworldly, especially holy mystic outside of ordinary time, but as a mysterious possibility for any lover of Jesus. Mechthild's book and others, like the works of German Dominican friar Henry Suso or Jan van Ruusbroec,

---

17. Frederick Dale Bruner, *The Gospel of John: A Commentary* (Grand Rapids: Eerdmans, 2012), 888.

were meant to guide other souls into the same kind of spiritual marriage to Christ. Such language can scandalize us—it reminds us that marriage to Christ is not merely corporate but also deeply individual, Godhead to person.

Medieval marriages to Jesus tended to follow a particular pattern, writes the scholar Rabia Gregory.[18] Medieval writers usually followed this set pattern because such depictions of Christ and the soul in love were seen as a spiritual or devotional path that other souls could follow to salvation. In discovering the longing that Christ has for each person, one will be reformed in love, believed writers like Mechthild and Suso. First, Jesus draws the soul near, inviting marriage. Sometimes there are traditional courtship rituals, like the exchange of letters or gifts, dancing, and feasting. A few events are consistent: Jesus usually crowns the soul with a glorious golden crown. The soul must undress in the presence of the bridegroom and then either be enrobed in greater beauty than before or nakedly meet in spiritual union.

Human union can be frightening, let alone divine union. Before my wedding, I remember shopping at a craft store with my mother. We were looking at ribbons to adorn the mason jar centerpieces for the reception (very 2010, I know). Under the fluorescent lights, fingering grosgrain of different shades and widths, I was suddenly struck by terror. I loved my now husband and was ready to marry him, but I, the introvert, thought, "I'll never be alone again." I wondered if I would lose some essential part of my personhood in my union with another. Marriage is not a commodity, not a pleasant product bought and sold, where I remain fundamentally singular and use marriage for my own advantages

---

18. See Gregory, *Marrying Jesus*, ch. 3, for in-depth consideration of variations on the marriage theme.

or foolishness. Actual union, the "one flesh" part that comes after the wedding and vows, is radical, transformative, and sure to change me if I let it. Would I be erased in this new intimacy and shared life?

I share these feelings with Margery Kempe, from one wedding to another, 2010 to 1414. Margery, clothed in dirty white, married but now celibate, mother of fourteen, presented an interesting challenge to every cleric she met. To the chagrin of many, she constantly and loudly wept in church (she called it roaring). Throughout her memoir-ish writings, she calls herself "this creature," which delightfully offers a taste of her wildness. On pilgrimage in Rome, at the Apostles' Church, she described a visionary moment:

> Also, the Father said to this creature [Margery], "Daughter, I will have thee wedded to my Godhead, for I shall show thee my secrets and my counsels, for thou shall dwell with me without end." Then the creature kept silent in her soul and answered not thereto, for she was full afraid of the Godhead and she knew no skill of the dalliance of the Godhead, for all her love and all her affection was set in the manhood of Christ and thereof she could understand well and she would not have parted from it for anything.[19]

Margery loved Jesus, concretely, bodily, passionately. She saw the form of Jesus in the male bodies she encountered in the streets of the Eternal City, often weeping uncontrollably when she saw a handsome man or even a cute baby because they shared his

---

19. *The Book of Margery Kempe*, ed. Lynn Staley (Kalamazoo, MI: Medieval Institute Publications, 1996), 35, lightly modernized by myself.

likeness. But even Margery was shocked at the idea of eternal marriage to the Godhead, Christ, the second person in the eternal fullness of the Trinity, rather than time traveling and marrying Christ's human, recognizably male body on earth.

Margery worried that she "knew no skill of the dalliance of the Godhead" because all her affection was attached to Christ's manhood. In Middle English, "dalliance" had a twofold meaning: It could indicate cultured, intimate, or spiritual conversation. It could also mean a sexual or sensual encounter.[20] If human marriage is a big deal, marriage to the Godhead is a shockingly big deal. What kinds of vulnerabilities, transformations, pains, and pleasures does one face in a divine marriage in its fullness? What is *dalliance* with the Godhead, the eternal, the utterly good and truthful and beautiful? Margery's silence is an understatement. She does readers the great favor of jolting us out of all complacency (or cheesiness) when we start to think about what it might mean to wed God.

Now we are finally back to Mechthild of Magdeburg, another bride of Christ. She was a Beguine, a member of a lay religious order who lived in a semimonastic community, who eventually joined a Cistercian nunnery. Among the first mystical writers to compose in medieval German, she wrote extensively of Jesus as a lover for each soul. Though her book, *The Flowing Light of the Godhead*, describes her own ecstatic experience as a lover of Jesus, she beckons others into divine marriage: "Dear friend, I have written for you this path of love. May God infuse it into your heart!

20. *Middle English Dictionary*, s.v. "dalliance (*n.*)," online edition in Middle English Compendium, ed. Frances McSparran et al. (Ann Arbor: University of Michigan Library, 2000–2018), accessed May 2022, https://quod.lib.umich.edu/m/middle-english-dictionary /dictionary/MED10503/track?counter=1&search_id=22699860.

Amen."[21] Mechthild depicts Lady Soul with Christ the bridegroom in conversation (Margery's *dalliance*!):

> "Stay, Lady Soul."
>
> "What do you bid me, Lord?"
>
> "Take off your clothes."
>
> "Lord, what will happen to me then?"
>
> "Lady Soul, you are so utterly formed to my nature
>
> That not the slightest thing can be between you and me.
>
> Never was angel so glorious
>
> That to him was granted for one hour
>
> What is given to you for eternity.
>
> And so you must cast off from you
>
> Both fear and shame and all external virtues."[22]

Mechthild first depicts the soul's fear at the aspect of true intimacy. Christ's love is not saccharine sweet, as if you're God's precious prince or princess. It is more like sex in the context of loving and consensual intimacy, as in marriage. Even in loving, trusting intimacy, the soul is apprehensive to fully reveal her limitations and sins and mistakes. Nakedness is risky; there's no hiding anything about yourself. In this unrobing, the soul casts off shame and embraces the vulnerability of desire.

Mechthild writes more of what happens when Christ surrenders himself to the soul, and the soul surrenders to Christ. Unrobing becomes a metaphor as Mechthild discards all guilt, worry, shame, and sorrow. The soul gives Jesus herself. She starts to taste sweetness as Christ gives her the gift and power of the Holy

---

21. Mechthild, *Flowing Light*, 62.
22. Mechthild, *Flowing Light*, 62.

Trinity that enters her soul and body. In this moment, she is given true wisdom, and she becomes weak in the power of this embrace. Jesus himself is lovesick. She longs to show him the depths of her faithfulness. She begins to receive the full knowledge of God as she "taste[s] with delight his love on her flesh. And then he begins to strengthen with holy feeling in her soul all his gifts."[23]

Generous lovers give and receive themselves in vulnerability. Note Mechthild's language, how it goes back and forth between Christ and the soul and their responses and their gifts. In giving and receiving, the soul is known in her fullness for the first time, as she begins to know the Godhead. In this union, there is mutual desire and submission, reciprocal surrender of strength and fortressed individuality, profound attention, naked truth, and finally, ecstasy. As with *Quia amore langueo*, the mutuality dispels highly gendered expectations of control and pleasure. In a medieval image of marriage and consummation like Mechthild's, one might expect to see what we today sometimes call "traditional" values—the person, as a representation of women or femininity, submits to Christ, and Christ, as himself, loves the person in return. Many models of Christian marriage present themselves as offering continuity with the past in teaching women as adoringly submissive, men as magnanimously loving, and each of those roles as fulfillment of a divine character. Not so for Mechthild. This spiritual consummation is not a one-sided, controlling act of pleasure, nor is it simply the submission of the bride to the bridegroom. While Christ is indeed magnanimously loving, he is also vulnerable, "lovesick," and he submits, humbles, and surrenders himself in echoes of the second chapter of Philippians. As in incarnation and crucifixion, Christ rejects power and control in order to love

23. Mechthild, *Flowing Light*, 227.

truly and freely. In that rejection of power and control in favor of vulnerability and intimacy comes the ecstatic joy of divine union with humanity, with the soul.

As Mechthild writes in wonder, even the angels do not share this union of joy with the Creator. This divine joy is almost embarrassingly hedonistic because there's no occasion for it but oneself, the soul learning to love.[24] I have not done anything worth such devotion, yet that joy in me remains, fundamentally creating, adoring, shaping, giving. In this ecstasy, whether in human or divine marriage, I can joyfully abandon my defenses. My body and soul are the site of holy union.

The Way of the Lover Is the Way of the Cross

You might be thinking that despite medieval insistence that you too could actually become a bride of Christ—that this bridal language is not only a metaphor for the corporate church—you've never had a mystical experience that sounds like Mechthild's or Margery's, and likely never will. I know I haven't. Are we meant to understand the ecstatic union of our souls with our Lover as something that happens only after our death or in the second coming?

It's not a mistake that the bridegroom is also a mysterious image of the apocalypse, of Christ's return in Revelation and in the Gospels. In Revelation 22:17, athirst with love, the bride calls, "Come!" to her bridegroom. I am struck by how our welcome of

---

24. I am thinking of Rowan Williams's beautiful essay on the grace of the body and sexual desire, "The Body's Grace," in *Theology and Sexuality: Classic and Contemporary Readings*, ed. Eugene F. Rogers (London: Wiley-Blackwell, 2002). In lovemaking, our bodies are "occasions for joy" and sites of profound vulnerability and risk.

our Lover balances out wholesome fear of the Judge. Certainly, we will not drink the fullness of union with Christ until his return. But medieval writers took this image—even in its strange, embodied ecstasy and joy—as transformative for us right now as we become more like our Lover.

My momentary terror in the ribbon aisle of the craft store was unnecessary, yet my instincts were right. I did not know what holy union would do to me, and I would change. Lovers become more like each other, from the silly to the serious. My husband did not like mushrooms when we got married; he now appreciates them on a pizza. I am braver as a result of his courage; he is more thoughtful because he married me. In our marriage to Jesus, he has already become like us in taking on human nature, and we become more like him in taking up the cross of love. Our joy in our Lover does not have to take the form of mystical glimpses of union with the Trinity. Right here and now, we are humbled and empowered in the ecstatic joy of recognizing the depths of Christ's passionate adoration of us.

Henri Nouwen wrote of the significance of ecstasy and joy for the church: "The ecstatic moment is precisely the moment when we lose our self-preoccupation and are drawn out of ourselves into a new reality."[25] I am often unbearably self-conscious and fearful of the naked exposure of my desire, like Mechthild's soul. In ecstatic joy, neighbor-love, God-love, and self-love all become more tangibly real because instead of bearing the crushing, defensive, and fearful expectations of what we should be, we can simply give of ourselves.

The way of Christ our Lover, as the lyric *Quia amore langueo* reminded us, is the way of the cross. We read in Matthew 16:24

---

25. Nouwen, *Lifesigns*, 75.

(NRSVA), "Jesus told his disciples, 'If any want to become my followers, let them deny themselves and take up their cross and follow me.'" In John 15, Jesus's beautiful invitation to make a home in his love and complete his joy precedes the lonely horror of Good Friday. The devotional books that sought out Jesus as a lover illustrate this idea in striking ways. In one medieval German prayer book, the Soul hangs on the cross while Christ comforts and supports her in her suffering. The facing picture depicts Christ tenderly undressing the Soul in preparation for divine union.

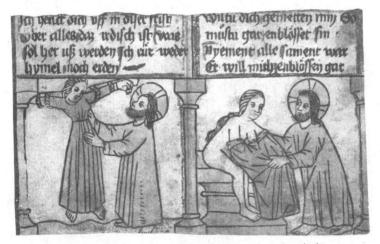

Christ supports the Soul on her cross; Christ tenderly undresses the Soul, *Christus unde die minnende Seele*, woodcut, ca. 1460, DG1930/198/6-7, Albertina, Vienna.

In a bizarre woodcut in a German prayer book, Christ calls out in German to the man to join him on the cross: "Son, give me your heart, I do not remit the punishment of one I hold dear." As he welcomes being pulled closer to Jesus, the man holds out his beating heart in trust and responds, "O Lord, this I want, I desire it, for this reason thus you should pull me."[26] Such an idea can be easily misapplied: *I will prove my love through suffering for you as you demand. You suffered so much for me, I had better suffer for you in punishment for my sins.* Medieval folks did sometimes understand it so. But following wise ones like Mechthild, or later saints like Teresa of Avila, who wrote of the pain of longing within the ecstasy of love, I understand the layering of the cross and the marriage bed as descriptive, not proscriptive.

Jesus Attracting the Faithful to Heart, hand-colored woodcut, ca. 1480/1490, 1943.3.853, Rosenwald Collection, National Gallery of Art, Washington, DC.

Public Domain.

In becoming Christ's faithful lover, we take up our cross of human vulnerability in giving our heart. Wholehearted love and

26. From the translation offered on the National Gallery website, https://www.nga.gov/collection/art-object-page.4070.html.

desire are hazardous to our basic equanimity. If our life goal is to avoid suffering, to love someone is a recipe for disaster. Desire is perilous and powerful. Love is as strong as death; many waters cannot quench it (Song of Songs 8:6–7). So we learn to love, to give our full selves to a grandparent, a first boyfriend, a beloved friend, a child, a spouse, or even a pet or a place, knowing that what awaits is the bliss of being known and chosen, and the creeping agony of possible rejection and certain death. The layering of the cross and the marriage bed portrays the highs and lows of a transformative union. In romantic comedies, it's the clichéd run through the airport. But in ordinary life, it's the dancing at weddings, the tending at the sickbed, the fidelity unto death.

In loving Jesus as our lover, we become more human, like the Son of Man himself. As Jesus says, as we make our home in his love, we are more touched by others' pain and joy. We are more open to the vulnerabilities and glories of being embodied souls (John 15:9–17). The way of the Lover is the way of the cross. Beyond the cross are resurrection and the mystery of true union.

Tarry not, dear spouse. The apples are ripe in the garden, and the table is set.

Meditation and Practices Inspired by Jesus the Lover

- Meditate on Jesus's words from the gospel of John:

    As the Father has loved me, so I have loved you; abide [make a home] in my love. If you keep my commandments, you will abide in my love, just as I have kept my Father's commandments and abide in his love. I have said these things to you so that my joy may be in you and that your joy may be complete.

This is my commandment, that you love one another as I have loved you. No one has greater love than this, to lay down one's life for one's friends. (John 15:9–13)

- Read the entire Song of Songs (it's pleasantly short). Read it as an allegory of Christ's love for yourself, as medieval people did, and see what emerges.
- Pay attention to your senses. The Song of Songs and medieval writers draw on images from nature, especially food, of blooming, beautiful fruitfulness. Bowls of wine, heaps of wheat, trees, mountains, pomegranates, saffron, and cinnamon describe the superabundance of the Lover's desire for us. Go on a walk and pay attention to the leaves and bark and flowers around you. If it's too cold or hot to go outside, next time you go to the grocery store, linger among the produce. Smell the fruits; attend to the colors and shapes. "Under the apple tree I awakened you," says the speaker of the Song (8:5).
- Listen to a love song, any kind. (I love Louis Armstrong's "La Vie en Rose," with the ecstatic trumpet solo.) How does it feel to be loved and desired? I know it's cheesy, but try to let go of self-consciousness and just enjoy being beloved by Jesus.

Prayer

O great dew of the noble Godhead,
O tender flower of the sweet maiden,

O beneficial fruit of the fair blossom,
O holy sacrifice of the Heavenly Father,
O faithful pledge of redemption for the whole world!
You, Lord, are my refreshment
And I am your blossoming.
You are small before me, Lord, in your submissiveness,
And I am great before you in the misery of my wickedness.
Daily I offer you whatever I have:
Nothing but baseness.
And you, Lord, shall infuse me with your grace.
Then I can flow from your love.

—Mechthild of Magdeburg[27]

---

27. Mechthild, *Flowing Light*, 195.

Chapter Four

The Knight

People generally lift their eyebrows with curiosity when I mention the medieval imagery of Jesus the Knight. For some, the thought of chivalry and knighthood evokes a past where knights sought good, fought evil, protected the downtrodden, and treated women with honor. Jesus as a knight sounds like Saint George slaying the dragon and rescuing the damsel in distress. For others (including myself), the idea of Jesus in armor inspires some queasiness. As a medievalist, I think of unholy crusades. What kind of knight can we consider Christ?

One of my favorite Middle English poems probes the idea of chivalry: *Sir Gawain and the Green Knight*. In this anonymous fourteenth-century poem, Gawain, a valiant and good-hearted young knight of King Arthur's Round Table, pursues a mysterious Green Knight who had appeared at Camelot and insulted Arthur's honor. Honor, essential to the system of chivalry that governs Arthur's court and Gawain's deepest convictions about the world, does not allow Gawain to let the insult pass. Instead, he enters into a game with the monstrous green man in which they promise to trade beheadings—and Gawain gets to behead the green man first. Unfortunately, the Green Knight simply will not die postbeheading. As the Green Knight gallops away, triumphantly cackling from his own head dangling from his high-held fist, he reminds the court that in a year's time Gawain must come find him for Gawain's own turn at the end of a shivery sharp axe blade.

Chivalry is everything to Gawain. But it comes in fourteenth-century forms: the poet spends a hundred lines of poetry describing Gawain's costly armor as Gawain sets out on his journey! A perfect knight is always from the nobility, with immaculate and beautiful armor. Gawain's shield particularly expresses his devotion to chivalric values. On one side is the Virgin Mary, and on the other is a symbol called the pentangle, a five-pointed star the poet calls "the endeles [endless] knot."[1] The five points each signify fivefold Gawain's character and values. First, his physical prowess is unmatched: He is "flawless" in his "five senses," and his "five fingers were never at fault."[2] His faith is anchored in Christ's five wounds on the cross. He finds his strength in the five joys of Mary in her son. And the last five are his most cherished values: *fraunchyse*, which means a particular kind of freedom and generosity associated with nobility and social status; fellowship; bodily purity; pity for those in lower social orders, women, or the suffering; and courtesy, which encompassed elaborate codes of manners for everything from the table to the bedroom.[3] These are the values of the most chivalric knight, which profoundly emphasize generosity, manners and social mores, the ability to take action when people with less power are in danger, and certain

---

1. *Sir Gawain and the Green Knight* in *The Poems of the Pearl Manuscript*, ed. Malcolm Andrew and Ronald Waldron, 5th ed. (Exeter, UK: University of Exeter Press, 2007), l. 630.

2. This snippet is from my favorite translation of *SGGK*, for those who wish to read for themselves. *Sir Gawain and the Green Knight*, trans. Simon Armitage (London: Faber & Faber, 2018), ll. 640–42. J. R. R. Tolkien also crafted a delightful version.

3. *Gawain*, ll. 651–55.

sexual behaviors. The endless knot weaves together Gawain's religious devotion, physical prowess, and knightly values seamlessly. So seamlessly that the poet ominously notes that if one part were taken out, the whole thing would collapse.

And it does. When Gawain the faultless inevitably fails this impossible code of chivalric pseudoreligion, the results are personally devastating. In an elaborate plot you'll have to read for yourself, he takes a supposedly magical green girdle offered by a beautiful woman and lies by omission to keep it and save his neck from the axe. The Green Knight gleefully catches him in the lie. Gawain survives the trap laid by the Green Knight but loses his identity as the perfect Christian knight. Before his eyes, Gawain's pentangle—his idealized chivalric version of himself—crumbles. Gawain's ugliest moment comes not at the moment of weakness, but afterward. In a frenzy of self-loathing, Gawain spews forth an impassioned speech blaming women as the source of all trouble since Eve—inadvertently revealing the shallowness of the values within his pentangle. The courteous treatment of women lasted only while times were good. And this is Gawain, whom we like and respect, whom the poet takes care to mark as the most chivalrous and genuinely devoted to his faith. What about all the real-life knights off on violent crusades or building up their fortunes through plunder and petty conflict?

Even at its best, chivalry was a value system that governed social order, gender relations, and the behavior of wealthy and powerful men. Our wise medieval poet knew, as Gawain did not, that chivalry and knighthood cannot be woven in *undifferentiated* with Christian ethics and identity. It is simply another system of values, used at times for good and at other times for evil. If Jesus is to be a knight in this chapter, he cannot follow the same path as Gawain, of simply being the best, most virtuous knight in all

Christendom. If we are to explore Christ himself as a knight, we must separate him from wealth and social nobility, from thinly disguised feelings of superiority over women and the poor, and from religious imagery in the service of violence, domination, and self-preservation.

Christ must be a different knight entirely.

The Barefoot Knight

Around the same time the *Gawain*-poet was composing his masterpiece, another Middle English poet, William Langland, was writing the complex allegorical poem *Piers Plowman*. The *Oxford English Dictionary* defines *allegory* as "a story which uses symbols to convey a hidden or ulterior meaning, typically a moral or political one ... an extended metaphor."[4] Allegory was central in the medieval imagination. Gregory the Great expands on his understanding of allegory from the last chapter:

> For allegory supplies the soul separated far from God with a kind of mechanism by which it is raised to God. By means of dark sayings in whose words a person can understand something of his own, he can understand what is not his to understand, and by earthly words he can be raised above the earth. Therefore, through means which are not alien to our way of understanding, that which is beyond our understanding can be known. By that which we do know—out of such are allegories made—divine meanings are clothed and through our

---

4. *Oxford English Dictionary*, s.v. "allegory (*n.*)," accessed August 2, 2021, https://www.oed.com/view/Entry/5230.

understanding of external speech we are brought to an inner understanding.[5]

In other words, Gregory believed that allegory is spiritually powerful. It raises human souls to comprehension of things divine, including difficult truths like the incarnation or the character of God. Otherworldly concepts are given form in next-door language, a style used by Jesus himself, the second person of the Trinity made man and come to dwell among us.

In the allegorical work *Piers Plowman*, Wille, whom today we would call the main character, experiences a series of dreams. These dreams are allegories for historical events, contemporary social issues, Scripture, and theology. All the "characters" of *Piers Plowman* are allegorical too. Consider Wille. His name indicates his simultaneous existence as, first, a person with the name William dreaming in the poem and, second, as the human "will" itself, undergoing spiritual transformation.

Toward the end of the poem, Wille falls asleep and witnesses something spectacularly beautiful: the events of Holy Week, set into allegory. Here comes Langland's version of the Christ-Knight:

> One . . . barefoot came riding bootless on an ass's back
> Without spurs or spear—sprightly he looked,
> As is natural for a knight who came to be dubbed,
> To get his gilt spurs and cut-away shoes.
> And then Faith was in a window and cried, *A, filii David!*
> As a herald of arms does when adventurous knights come
>   to jousts.

---

5. Gregory the Great, *Exposition of the Song of Songs*, in Denys Turner, *Eros and Allegory: Medieval Exegesis of the Song of Songs* (Kalamazoo, MI: Cistercian, 1995), 217.

> Old Jews of Jerusalem sang for joy,
>> *Blessed is he that cometh in the name of the Lord.*
>> (XX.8–16)[6]

Langland creatively blends the sounds and events of Palm Sunday with a knight coming to joust in a tournament. The allegorical figure of Faith acts as a herald of arms, the medieval version of a sports announcer. Wille is perplexed:

> Then I asked Faith what all this activity meant,
> And who should joust in Jerusalem? "Jesus," he said,
> "And fetch what the Fiend claims, the fruit of Piers the
>> plowman."
> ... *Liberium-dei-arbitrium* has for love undertaken
> That this Jesus for his gentility will joust in Piers' armor,
> In his helmet and in his mail, *humana natura* ...
>> (XX.17–22)

The reader meets a word picture of the incarnation: Jesus clad in human nature, jousting in the "armor" of a simple plowman against the Fiend and all the powers of death.

Some context here helps us to recapture the strangeness of Langland's image. Medieval thinkers often conceived of their society as divided into three estates: the nobles and gentry, the clergy, and the peasants. Each of these estates had its essential role in society. The clergy were "those who prayed," the folks who provided spiritual instruction, interceded for their communities, and administered the sacraments. The peasants were "those who

---

6. *William Langland's Piers Plowman: The C Version*, trans. George Economou (Philadelphia: University of Pennsylvania Press, 1996).

labored," the essential group who grew, cultivated, and harvested food for everyone. A plowman would have belonged to this estate, as his main job was tilling and tending the crops that fed England. And the nobles were "those who fought," the lords of society who were supposed to protect the realm from invaders, administer justice locally, and use their ample largesse to support the poor and the church in their community. Knights belonged to this last estate. Most people took these divisions of medieval society for granted. John Wycliffe, the Oxford theologian who caused so much trouble for the fourteenth-century institutional church, claimed that God founded the three estates and compared them to the Trinity.[7] Most medieval thinkers agreed with him (in this case).

These estates stayed separate. Peasants did not become nobles, and nobles certainly did not want to be peasants. Knights would have curled their lips in disgust at the thought of clothing themselves in a plowman's garb. Imagine what people would think today if a powerful executive showed up to her elegant Manhattan office in the dusty clothes and boots of a construction worker. Like a CEO donning a power suit for an important meeting, knights came to battle in their best armor, arms displayed so all would know their identity and their great deeds of prowess.

In works of literature, as in the tales of King Arthur's court, and sometimes in actual tournaments as part of a courtly game of illusion, knights would occasionally disguise themselves.[8] But they

---

7. John Wycliffe, "The Clergy May Not Hold Property," in *The English Works of Wyclif, Hitherto Unprinted*, ed. F. D. Matthew, EETS, O.S. 74 (London, 1880), 362; quoted in Joseph A. Dane, "The Three Estates and Other Medieval Trinities," *Florilegium* 3.1 (1981): 283–309, https://doi.org/10.3138/flor.3.013.

8. See, for example, the elaborate games of knightly disguise in the *Morte Darthur*, the fifteenth-century bestseller by Thomas Malory.

certainly would not have dressed like plowmen. To dress in all black armor provoked mystery, curiosity, and interest. To dress in dirty old peasant clothes and to sit barefoot on the back of a donkey would have elicited judgment and disgust. Gawain would never have dressed so!

Langland's knight comes to fight a holier battle, one that ultimately eschews the typical knightly trappings of wealth and violence. The Christ-Knight is still committed to providing defense, salvation, and justice to those at the mercy of their enemies. But this knight dressed in plowman's garb demonstrates God's radical, division-destroying humility and love in his embodiment as Jesus.

Jesus the Knight Redeems Our Labor

Jesus the Knight comes to fetch the fruit of Piers the Plowman from the grasp of Satan and death itself. But for us to truly understand the character of Jesus the Knight, we must first learn about Piers the Plowman and his fruit. In this part of Langland's work, he represents humanity *and* the backbreaking labor of living well after the fall. In the image of fruit, we can find the people of God. Consider all the harvest and planting parables about human souls in Jesus's teachings: Jesus redeems people, his fullest harvest. Fruit also can mean the results of the labors of humanity. The curse of Genesis led to the horrifically difficult labor of living in the world, of feeding oneself and giving birth and loving well. Jesus the Knight does not just redeem people, he also baptizes their work.

Langland's inclusion of human labor in his allegory drew attention to the plight of real English laborers. Laborers were suffering under wage restrictions in the wake of the plague that decimated the population. In many places, unjust legislation kept them as little better than enslaved people.[9] They simply were not appreciated by the society that depended on them to eat. When I encounter these lines, I too feel convicted. How little do my society and I consider the workers who tend, harvest, and prepare our food?

Medieval laborers faced terrible challenges in their production of the food that fed Europe. At the time, a popular war strategy in France and England was the *chevauchée*. To win a war, an army or group of knights would deplete enemy resources by burning and pillaging the villages that fed them. Most medieval cities and towns had walls to protect them from invaders, but little rural villages did not. Peasants often bore the ultimate costs of war. They were killed or assaulted, their homes were destroyed, and the fruits of their backbreaking work went up in greedy flames or were stolen by their killers.

In *Piers Plowman*, the Christ-Knight has come to save these poor workers, in contrast to the Fiend and his knights of death who would destroy both their bodies and their labor. Langland reminds us that Jesus comes for all kinds of workers. Despite his knightly status, Jesus works for the redemption of all estates, knight and farmworker together preserved and transformed. The Christ-Knight in his plowman's clothes recalls us to the suffering of the oppressed in our midst today.

While Langland's Knight calls readers to face the suffering of literal laborers, especially oppressed workers, he also reminds readers of the significance and redemption of all material and spiritual labor, from the menial to the great.

For we all have labors. Right now, my daily work as a writer

---

9. Juliet Barker, *1381: The Year of the Peasants' Revolt* (Cambridge, MA: Belknap Press of Harvard University Press, 2014) gives a picture of the unsettled, oppressive conditions that led to the violent uprising of peasants in 1381, during which Langland lived.

and stay-at-home mother consists of work enjoyable, dull, and frustrating. I change a lot of diapers. I wipe a lot of bottoms. I discipline. I have to practice controlling my temper as I monitor yet another tantrum thrown in public. On a macro and micro level, parenting necessitates a degree of unpleasant labor, often invisible or unappreciated. However, changing a diaper promptly is the right thing to do. Practicing a firm, patient, and loving response in the face of an embarrassing public meltdown costs me a satisfying burst of anger but values my kid. We tangibly love through small but costly acts.

Many people practice even costlier acts of love. Perhaps you care for an ill or disabled family member or pay the bills by working an unenjoyable job. These decisions and actions aren't ideal, yet at different moments in life, they may be right. And they can be very challenging. They can cost us fun, solitude, adventures, friendships, or careers.

Sometimes we think that unless things are easy, we are doing something wrong or life isn't as it should be. Sometimes this awareness—that something isn't as it should be because it is difficult—is true: some relationships should not work out, some jobs need to be left behind, some boundaries must be drawn to protect and heal our bodies and minds. But sometimes *living well is just hard*. Many Americans have a strange cultural belief that we can eliminate laborious suffering through technology, education, or lawmaking. This belief that suffering can and should be abolished can lead us into self-deception. The simple day-to-day tasks of running a house, going to work, caring for children, and taking care of one's body and mind can feel burdensome. But all virtues are usually arduous. To completely purge living well of its daily difficulty is neither possible nor desirable in the transformative, real work of caring for one another. Laboring in the field of life to bring forth the fruits of community, of a healthy self, of caring for the poor, the oppressed, and the brokenhearted is often difficult. Langland reminds us that Jesus joyfully redeems not only ourselves but also our daily, costly labors.

Yet at other times, we are merely surviving after a spiritual or material *chevauchée*. All efforts have been torched by enemies within and without. Living can feel like death. Thankfully, Jesus the Knight doesn't just ride in to shouts of acclaim on Palm Sunday or stride away triumphantly after slaying the dragon. Palm Sunday leads to the crucifixion and its requisite, awful courage of endurance. After Jesus's barefoot arrival at the joust, Langland portrays a medieval doctrine called the harrowing of hell, in which we witness Jesus tearing down the gates of damnation and scattering the enemies of life.

Jesus the Knight Goes through Hell

The harrowing of hell is an ancient belief that after Jesus died but before he rose from the grave, he drank the cup of human death down to its bitter dregs. He literally went to hell. In the Apostles' Creed, many Christians still recite, "He descended into hell." But many, especially Protestants, understand this descent as a metaphor for his experience of death. Sometimes they replace this line with "He descended into death." But medieval people did not believe the harrowing of hell was metaphorical. Jesus did not bypass a single part of the human death, not even the darkness of Sheol.

This is how Langland described the harrowing: A distant beacon appears in the half-light of hell. The demons speculate on what it could be. They wait in trepidation as the Light draws closer. At last the Light, blindingly brilliant in the smog, arrives at hell's gates. The demons can't see who is at the heart of the starry brightness. And Lucifer dares to call out,

> "What lord are you?" asked Lucifer. A voice said aloud:
> "The lord of might and main, that made all things.
> Dukes of this dim place, undo these gates now
> That Christ may come in, the son of heaven's king."
>   And with that breath hell with all of Belial's
>   bars broke;
> Despite all prevention, the gates were wide open.
> Patriarchs and prophets, *populus in tenebris*,
>   [people in darkness]
>   Sang with Saint John, "*Ecce agnus dei!*"
>   [Behold the Lamb of God!] (XX.360–367)

Behold the Lamb of God! All the people of the old law are freed as the gates are broken. The harrowing of hell teaches that Jesus also redeemed those who came before him in his descent. Langland evoked the prophet Isaiah in this depiction: The people in darkness have seen a great light. The patriarchs and prophets sing with ecstasy.

Then Wille wakes up from his vision of the history of salvation. It is Easter morning in his own world. Filled with joy, he calls his wife and daughter to join the community of saints on earth at his own parish church and participates in the liturgy celebrating Christ's resurrection. Come and creep to the cross, he cries out to his family.

There are different species of joy. There is quiet, contemplative joy, the kind generated by sitting near a cozy fireplace with a great book, holding hands with a beloved, listening to the ocean.

And there's sparkling, wild joy. It is the joy that small children
have when they eat ice cream and then run around afterward, losing their minds in the delight of the sugar rush. It is the joy that
one experiences in the reception of unforeseen good news, when
unexpected healing from illness occurs, when the ball swooshes
through the hoop at the very last moment, when you meet unexpectedly with old friends and the words refuse to stop bubbling up.
This joy generates action—dancing, laughing, shrieking, singing,
and doing things. Outside of childhood, this joy can be quite rare.

Langland's image of the barefoot knight descending into hell
and saving the people in darkness evokes this latter joy. Death
itself no longer has the last word. The dragon is dead! Our cham-
pion Christ has destroyed our ancient enemy! The gates of hell
crumble into dust as the Light of the World falls upon them. One
can hear the drumbeat of victory in the verses of the fifteenth-
century Scottish poet William Dunbar:

> Done is the battle on the dragon black!
> Our champion, Christ, confounded his force.
> The gates of hell are broken with a crack;
> The sign triumphal raised is the Cross.[10]

Sharing in the Courage and Joy of Jesus the Knight

Many hundreds of years later, one of my favorite writers (and a
medievalist himself), J. R. R. Tolkien, wrote a scene in *The Return*

10. William Dunbar, "A Hymn of the Resurrection," in *Medieval English Lyrics: A Critical Anthology*, ed. R. T. Davies (Evanston, IL: Northwestern University Press, 1964), 253. Lightly translated by myself.

of the King that feels inspired by these themes of Jesus as a knight. A gigantic army endowed with the powers of evil besieges the one center of human power left in Middle-earth, the city of Gondor. Sun and sky are hidden in the darkness of their enemies, and it is the captain of despair himself, the deathless and evil Nazgul king, who leads the fight against the city. Leaderless, awash in corpses, the smoldering city waits for its inevitable fall. But Gondor does not know that warriors from the neighboring kingdom of Rohan have secretly ridden to their aid. Now we see what happens through the eyes of Merry the hobbit, riding with the king of Rohan:

> The king sat upon Snowmane, motionless, gazing upon the agony of Minas Tirith, as if stricken suddenly by anguish, or by dread. He seemed to shrink down, cowed by age. Merry himself felt as if a great weight of horror and doubt had settled upon him. His heart beat slowly. Time seemed poised in uncertainty. They were too late! Too late was worse than never!
>
> Then suddenly Merry felt it at least, beyond doubt: a change. Wind was in his face! Light was glimmering. Far, far away, in the South the clouds could be dimly seen as remote gray shapes, rolling up, drifting: morning lay beyond them. . . .
>
> At that sound the bent shape of the king sprang suddenly erect. Tall and proud he seemed again; and rising in his stirrups he cried in a loud voice, more clear than any there had ever heard a mortal man achieve before:
>
> > *Arise, arise, Riders of Theoden!*
> > *Fell deeds awake: fire and slaughter!*
> > *spear shall be shaken, shield be splintered,*
> > *a sword day, a red day, ere the sun rises!*
> > *Ride now, ride now! Ride to Gondor!*

... His golden shield was uncovered, and lo! it shone like an image of the Sun, and the grass flamed into green about the white feet of his steed. For morning came, morning and a wind from the sea; and darkness was removed, and the hosts of Mordor wailed, and terror took them, and they fled, and died, and the hoofs of wrath rode over them.[11]

King Théoden, called forward to what will be his death, lingers in uncertainty and fear. Readers know that Théoden's age and life experiences have damaged him. He was unprepared for the violent forces of evil at Rohan's doorstep. But suddenly inspired by otherworldly courage, the magic of Gandalf the wizard's resistance, he rides forward as an emissary of light into the darkness.

Tolkien's stories sweep me into a strange mixture of longing, relief, and fiery joy. What I love about fantasy writing is that it takes up these moments of hopeless horror in a different setting than our real world. It reveals the courage and beauty that we would find difficult to see when we suffer despair in our ordinary lives, as we face the hospital bed, loneliness, grief, systemic racism, poverty.

So it is when medieval poets envision Jesus the Knight. Unimaginable courage and unforeseen joy characterize the Christ-Knight. Jesus jousting his ancient enemy without weapons. Jesus descending alone into utter darkness. Jesus stripping the ancient gates of terror to their foundations. Jesus the Knight holds these moments of courage and joy together. He models the courage and joy that humanity needs in the difficulties and varieties of our labor. When I read, from John of Grimestone's preaching book,

---

11. J. R. R. Tolkien, *The Return of the King* (Boston: Houghton Mifflin, 1994), 819–20.

"I am Jesu that come to fight / Withouten shield and spear,"[12] it thrills me to my marrow. The words provide a glimpse of radical courage beyond warranted hope. I recognize the bravery of fighting a battle without a shield or spear in figures like Corrie ten Boom, Martin Luther King Jr., Dietrich Bonhoeffer, and Saint Óscar Romero. And like Jesus the Knight, the courage of the last three in the pursuit of justice led to their martyrdoms.

Are we seriously asked to practice the courage of Jesus the Knight? Yes and no. Not all are called to be martyrs like King, Bonhoeffer, and Romero. Not all are knights, come to fight without shield and spear. Everyone has different gifts. Yet each of us is called to practice courage as an aspect of the character of Jesus.

Ordinary people do not romantically ride into battle against all odds. Most of us do not have the guts or skills of the heroes I just listed. It can be difficult to conceptualize courage. Medieval writers and thinkers usually used the word *fortitude* instead of courage, which they included as one of the "cardinal" virtues (cardinal meaning "hinge" in Latin). Our actions hinge on them, like a door swinging open. The way a door opens, its ease of opening and the direction it moves, largely depends on its hinges. Saint Thomas Aquinas provides a useful definition of *fortitude* in his *Summa Theologiae*. According to Aquinas, all virtues aid the will to follow the path of right living as people discern rightness through their God-given reason. Sometimes an obstacle hinders the will from living well. This is where fortitude enters the picture. Fortitude—of the mind, the body, or both, depending on the obstacle—enables someone to remove that daunting obstacle.[13] I particularly love a definition from Saint Augustine of Hippo. He wrote, "Fortitude is love bearing all things readily for the sake of the beloved."[14] His version of fortitude is spacious and welcoming, harboring all kinds of costly actions of love under the banner of courage.

The abundant flexibility of the virtues has been largely forgotten today. We often think of a virtue as a rule or a demand, a one-size-fits-all way of thinking about good behavior that is outdated or irrelevant now. But the virtues richly expand and contract to fit individual lives. Fortitude is not formulaic in any sense; it can take many shapes and characterize many types of action. The classic image of courage is the knight, a soldier in battle laying down his life. But most of us are not soldiers, nor are we members of a persecuted secret church or any other obvious sphere of courage. But a high school student going to introduce himself to another student sitting alone may exercise fortitude in his choice to love a lonely fellow student at the cost of his image. C. S. Lewis used a wonderful illustration to illuminate the wide range of actions that could characterize fortitude:

> Human beings judge one another by their external actions. God judges them by their moral choices. When a neurotic who has a pathological horror of cats forces himself to pick up a cat for some good reason, it is quite possible that in God's eyes he

---

13. Thomas Aquinas, *Summa Theologiae*, trans. Laurence Shapcote, ed. John Mortensen and Enrique Alarcon (Lander, WY: Aquinas Institute for the Study of Sacred Doctrine, 2012), *ST* II.II.58.1.corp, (hereafter cited as *ST*).

14. Saint Augustine, *On the Morals of the Catholic Church*, trans. Richard Stothert, from *Nicene and Post-Nicene Fathers, First Series*, vol. 4, ed. Philip Schaff (Buffalo, NY: Christian Literature, 1887). Revised and edited for New Advent by Kevin Knight, accessed April 21, 2021, http://www.newadvent.org/fathers/1401.htm.

has shown more courage than a healthy man may have shown in winning the [Victoria Cross].[15]

Lewis helpfully distinguished between the outward aspect and outcome of an action and its inward choice and direction. When we think of the virtues, context matters. A soldier may leap into battle through unthinking adrenaline or through the pleasure of risk-taking. That terrifying and often admirable act does not necessarily make her courageous, it merely reveals her as daring and sometimes even foolhardy if the cause is not worthy or the risk too great. In contrast, a small, seemingly inconsequential action, like picking up a cat or speaking to a stranger, may hide great fortitude.

Moreover, fortitude does not entail that the courageous action has been done unthinkingly or without fear and struggle. I've caught myself telling my young children, "You're so brave!" when they fall down and cry for only a moment. While it's good to learn not to milk your ever-so-slightly scraped knee for attention or needlessly complain about minor issues, my praise reveals a paucity in our cultural understanding of courage. It has become a stoic virtue, overly associated with a particular cultural masculinity. In every action movie, the hero gets wounded and keeps going against all odds, blood dripping down his chiseled torso while he gives it nary a second thought. Bravery doesn't cry; it clenches its square jaw and does the impossible even when mortally wounded. This is a severely limited portrait of fortitude. Jesus wept and sweat in the garden of Gethsemane before the horror and enormous courage of assenting to his arrest, torture, and death in the name of love.

Some of the greatest acts of fortitude are thrust upon us in the form of our bodily infirmities, in sickness and aging and

---

15. C. S. Lewis, *Mere Christianity* (San Francisco: HarperSanFrancisco, 2001), 91.

weakness. As Thomas Aquinas said, it "also belongs to fortitude to bear bravely with the infirmities of the flesh."[16] He categorized patience and endurance under this form of courage. I witness fortitude in my aging grandmother who, despite not being able to eat many kinds of food and left with permanent digestive and throat issues from a botched surgery, takes a walk every day to care for her body and still volunteers to provide for the needy in her parish. I see it in my other grandmother, steadfastly and patiently caring for her terminally ill husband through a pandemic. I observed it in my mother, diagnosed with an unusual type of cancer and forced to make all kinds of confusing decisions as doctors disagreed on what it was. I marvel at it in my sister, clinically depressed for most of her life, accepting being on medication to be healthy enough to love herself, her husband, and her community. These women all participate in the fortitude of Jesus the Knight, at times with few tears and at other times with many. Fortitude can illuminate an ordinary life at sudden moments, but most of the time it is a practice hidden from the casual observer. *Fortitude is love bearing all things readily for the sake of the beloved.*

And then of course there are the Romeros, the Bonhoeffers, the ten Booms, and the Kings, practicing the fortitude of the crucifixion: a lightning-bolt fortitude that dazzles, frightens, and costs everything in the battle against the massive enemies of inequity, poverty, racism, ecological disaster, and political corruption. As Christians, we are called to care about these things: to tend to the oppressed, the lonely, the poor, the imprisoned, the strangers in a strange land. The figure of Jesus the Knight, both Langland's version and Dunbar's, reminds us of Jesus's courage and the joy of his redemption of each of us and our often backbreaking,

---

16. Aquinas, *ST II*.II.123.1.

heartbreaking, *dis-couraging* work in the world. Shame may keep us from acknowledging where we have not worked justice, mercy, or compassion. Fear or hopelessness may keep us from action. In the face of such massive and daunting problems, it is easy to feel drained of all courage. But in the figure of Jesus the Knight, at work to redeem all laborers and their labors, on his way to fight a seemingly hopeless battle, *we are encouraged*. Think about the breakdown of the word *encourage*: en-courage. To fill with courage, to animate, to inspire, the *Oxford English Dictionary* notes.[17] Langland's Christ-Knight reminds us that we are redeemed through his courage, and moreover, our labors matter so much that Christ redeems them too. You matter, and how you act and what you work in the world also matter, regardless of how little your power feels in comparison with the present darkness.

Meditation and Practices Inspired by Jesus the Knight

- Meditate on Ephesians 6:10–17. What stands out to you? What particular armor do you need right now?

> Finally, be strong in the Lord and in the strength of his power; put on the whole armor of God, so that you may be able to stand against the wiles of the devil, for our struggle is not against blood and flesh but against the rulers, against the authorities, against the cosmic powers of this present darkness, against the spiritual forces of

---

17. *Oxford English Dictionary*, s.v. "encourage (*v.*)," accessed August 2, 2021, https://www.oed.com/view/Entry/61791?rskey=Ptjak2&result=2#eid.

evil in the heavenly places. Therefore take up the whole armor of God, so that you may be able to withstand on the evil day and, having prevailed against everything, to stand firm. Stand, therefore, and belt your waist with truth and put on the breastplate of righteousness and lace up your sandals in preparation for the gospel of peace. With all of these, take the shield of faith, with which you will be able to quench all the flaming arrows of the evil one. Take the helmet of salvation and the sword of the Spirit, which is the word of God.

- *Done is the battle on the dragon black!* Christ has risen from the tomb! This week, celebrate something. Participate in a distant echo of the joy of the resurrected Christ-Knight. Eat cake or have a glass of wine with a friend. Do something small: paint your nails a bold color, or watch a YouTube video of your sports team's triumphant moment. Relish joy intentionally.
- William Langland's Christ-Knight comes to redeem the labors of the oppressed. If you have not yet practiced the action from the "Judge" chapter—building a habit of being a neighbor—be en-couraged by Jesus the Knight and add a practice to combat oppression in your community (see the practices from the "Judge" chapter for ideas!).
- Sometimes it is easier to take heart from fantastical or historical books and movies than from daily life. To inspire fortitude, read or watch *The Lord of the Rings* by J. R. R. Tolkien; or with kids, read Madeleine L'Engle's Time Quintet, or watch *The Sound of Music* or Marvel's *Black Panther*. For more historical choices, *The King's Speech*, *Of Gods and Men*, and *Hidden Figures* are great options.

There are many inspiring, courageous movies and books out there that crack open the idea of courage and liberate it from stereotypes.

Prayer

Jesus the Knight, share your courage and strength with me. Help me to pray for and serve your children oppressed by the powers of sin, whether they're oppressed through greed, ignorance, racism, sexism, or any kind of prejudice or discrimination. Provide ways for me to meaningfully aid your suffering people. En-courage me, Jesus who fights without shield or spear.

Jesus the Knight, I remember your fortitude as I face battles in my own life. I name these battles: [illness, family conflict, prejudice, exhaustion, finances, loneliness]. Help me to lay down my human weapons and let you, the God armored in human nature, fight these wars that are so painful. Through fortitude, empower me to seek help when I need it and to endure adversity with your patience.

Jesus the Knight, fill me with joy as I remember your triumphant resurrection. Give me the eyes to see your redemption in the world and your present and coming victory over all evil. I am thankful that death is not the final word. Thank you for fighting for me and for all who struggle and suffer. In Jesus's name. Amen.

Chapter Five

The Word

In *Harry Potter and the Chamber of Secrets*, Harry, the magical hero of J. K. Rowling's series, frightens his bullying cousin, Dudley, with some magical-sounding words that he insists will set the hedge on fire. "*Jiggery pokery!*" Harry fiercely whispers. "*Hocus pocus!*" Dudley is horrified, thinking Harry is doing real magic, and we readers smile because we get the joke—Harry uses words that aren't really magical but sound like they might be. They are the ineffectual shadow of true magic.

Hocus pocus has a fascinating backstory. In the medieval Latin celebration of the Eucharist, the Mass, the anointed priest lifted the unleavened bread before the eyes of the people and proclaimed, *Hoc est corpus meum*, "This is my body," the words spoken by Christ in the Gospels. These are the words of institution, sometimes simply called *verba*, "the words"; in their utterance and by the grace of God, the round, white wafer becomes the sacred body of Jesus. Now say those words out loud quickly: *hoc est corpus*. Do they sound familiar? Many believe *hoc est corpus meum*, at some point after the Reformation, perhaps morphed into *hocus pocus*, nonsense words of play magic. Was *hocus pocus* meant to belittle the Eucharistic rite as superstitious? Was it a misinterpretation from non-Latin-speaking laity? Or was it meant to humorously echo the weightiest words one could think of as one playacted power onstage or in jest? No one knows.

Though the mystery of the Eucharist displayed the potency of language, it wasn't the only example of the reverence in which many medieval people held the spoken and written word. *Glamour*, an old word for dazzling magic, comes from *grammar*, the medieval study of words and how they work.[1] In the late Middle Ages, a new, popular feast day came into prominence: the Feast of the Holy Name of Jesus, celebrating the power of Christ's name itself as word. Words held the power to curse and destroy. Words held the power to create, given that God spoke the universe into reality from nothing. Christ himself is named *Verbum* in Latin, *Logos* in Greek, the Word in the opening of John's gospel.

Hocus pocus may be a ghostly remnant of *hoc est corpus*, yet the difference between the two instructs us. One phrase takes place in a particular context (Mass, at a specific moment in time and history, in a church), spoken by a particular person (an anointed and trained priest), and carries utmost power (the transformation of unleavened bread into God's salvific body). The other has no particular context or efficacy—that's the whole point. Even in a book about wizards, *hocus pocus* is about look and sound. It's form without function. It seems like magic, but it's gibberish. It can be said by anyone anywhere at any time in any place because it has been emptied of meaning.

Setting aside our specific beliefs about the Eucharist, in Western modernity, Christians have generally become more of a *hocus pocus* people than a *hoc est corpus* people. By that, I mean

1. *Merriam-Webster Online*, s.v. "glamour (*n.*)," accessed January 2023, https://www.merriam-webster.com/dictionary/glamour.

that Western Christians no longer belong to a broader culture in which words are explicitly understood as vehicles of power shaped by their form and context, "glamorous" and perilous. On social media, from the stages of political rallies, in ubiquitous advertisements, even person to person, we throw around language as if it does nothing, as if only our right to speak whatever we wish matters. Even cruel or plain stupid words are "only" words, *hocus pocus* nonsense. "I didn't really *mean* it," we say. Yet as anyone knows who has listened to a racist screed or degrading "locker room talk," made marriage vows, or said "I love you," words still hold real power. There's no truth to the childhood rhyme, "Sticks and stones may break my bones, but words will never hurt me." Even *hocus pocus* scares Dudley Dursley. Yet when reminded of the true potency of language and the need for care, context, and subtlety, we often sputter and retreat in anger, defensiveness, or even fear.

Medieval theologians argued that disordered speech was a reckless path into heresy, into speaking lies about God and ourselves that we end up believing.[2] While the rest of this book focuses mostly on word pictures about Jesus, this chapter explores words about the Word themselves, the ordered shape of language about God that we now call the *Summa Theologiae*, the premier text of scholastic theology. This ordered shape becomes its own word picture through which we glimpse medieval understanding of Christ's character. In his great theological teaching project, Saint Thomas Aquinas teaches readers to put our God-talk in order so that we may fittingly teach and imitate incarnational love in how we speak of Christ.

As we order our God-talk, we enter into Aquinas's theology via

---

2. Thomas Aquinas, *Summa Theologiae*, trans. Laurence Shapcote, ed. John Mortensen and Enrique Alarcon (Lander, WY: Aquinas Institute for the Study of Sacred Doctrine, 2012), III.16.8.corp, attributed originally to Jerome (hereafter cited as *ST*).

the highly ordered context and structure or form of the *Summa*, and then dip our toes into scholasticism as we meditate on the relationship between language and incarnation. ·

Scholasticism, Thomas Aquinas, and the *Summa*

Scholasticism leaves many with a bad taste in their mouths, probably not helped by the grand-sounding name. Scholasticism is simply the theology of the *schola*, of the universities just beginning in twelfth- and thirteenth-century Europe. Scholastic theology was written and taught in Latin across Europe by men like Peter Abelard, Duns Scotus, Thomas Aquinas, and William of Ockham.[3] Famously complex, the theological mode possesses a formidable Latin vocabulary that makes it challenging to crack open and read without significant training or guidance.

Saint Thomas Aquinas was born in 1225 in Roccasecca, near the Italian town of Aquino. When he was only five, his aristocratic family placed him in the nearby Benedictine monastery. They expected that perhaps he would eventually become its abbot. Teenage Thomas rebelled from this respectable path and joined the Dominicans, the alarming new order of preaching friars founded by the Spaniard Saint Dominic only a few decades earlier. The Dominicans practiced voluntary poverty—they desired to imitate Christ by rejecting all worldly possessions, preached from town to town, and lived on alms alone. They were shaking up the medieval order of religious life.

---

3. The use of *men* is deliberate; women could not attend universities before the nineteenth and twentieth centuries.

Cue the panic in Aquinas's patrician family. They locked him in his room at the family castle and employed some questionable strategies to tempt him from his Dominican vocation. At one point, his brothers supposedly sent a prostitute into his room to remind him of what he was missing in his vows of celibacy. According to tradition, he chased her out of the room with a fiery brand he had grabbed from the fireplace, then he drew a cross on the door with ash. Poor woman! The family recognized their defeat.

Most of us probably consider Aquinas an establishment theologian, given his current status as perhaps the most important theologian in Roman Catholicism. But that wasn't always the case. Aquinas was unusual. Toward the end of the theologian's life, he was shockingly writing "the equivalent in volume to two or three average-length novels per month."[4] He died amid controversy over how he used the writings of Muslim interpreters of Aristotle to argue his theological points. The bishop of Paris even condemned to be burned some of Aquinas's writings in 1277, just a few years after his death. One should not fall into the trap of mistaking him for status quo.

Aquinas wrote his masterpiece, the *Summa Theologiae*, as a theological treatise for his Dominican brothers *beginning* to learn scholastic theology. The work is split into three large parts, called the Prima Pars, Secunda Pars, and Tertia Pars (simply, the first, second, and third parts). Each part consists of a series of questions, composed of other questions, that naturally lead from one to the next. If you asked yourself, "What does Jesus, the Word Incarnate, look like in the wordiest of discourses, scholasticism?" you would

---

4. Denys Turner, *Thomas Aquinas: A Portrait* (New Haven: Yale University Press, 2013), 41.

first crack open the Tertia Pars, the part explicitly about Christ, and read its first question:

> Question 1: The Fitness of the Incarnation
> 1. Whether it was fitting that God should become incarnate?
> 2. Whether it was necessary for the restoration of the human race that the word of God should become incarnate?
> 3. Whether, if man had not sinned, God would have become incarnate?
> 4. Whether God became incarnate to take away actual sin, rather than to take away original sin?
> 5. Whether it was fitting that God should have become incarnate in the beginning of the human race?
> 6. Whether the incarnation ought to have been put off till the end of the world?[5]

These questions are definitely for beginners, right? When I first opened the *Summa*, I felt overwhelmed and, quite honestly, put off. The audacity, even impossibility of questions like these took my breath away; I even felt a little scared of them. Aquinas possessed an eagerness for truth through words, unimpeded by fears that the answer would not be what one hopes it is, wants it to be, or thinks it should be—or even that the answer would truly conclude the question.[6] Aquinas's Jesus, we first discover, is a Jesus big enough for questions.

---

5. *ST III*.1.

6. I love the words of Turner from *Aquinas*: "Thomas is intellectually braver, even perhaps more irresponsible; there are for him questions that have to be asked, but cannot be answered," (135).

What Comes before Answers?

Let's look together at Aquinas's answer to the first question within this block of questions in the third part of the *Summa*, "Whether it was fitting that God should become incarnate?":

> To each thing, that is befitting which belongs to it by reason of its very nature; thus to reason befits man, since this belongs to him because he is of a rational nature. But the very nature of God is goodness, as is clear from Dionysus (Div. Nom. I). Hence, what belongs to the essence of goodness befits God. But it belongs to the essence of goodness to communicate itself to others, as is plain from Dionysus (Div. Nom. IV). Hence it belongs to the essence of the highest good to communicate itself in the highest manner to the creature, and this is brought about chiefly by *His so joining created nature to Himself that one Person is made up of these three—the Word, a soul, and flesh*, as Augustine says (De Trin. XIII). Hence it is manifest that it was fitting that God should become incarnate.[7]

To rephrase briefly, Aquinas notes that the very nature of God is goodness. As another theologian, Pseudo-Dionysius, had argued, goodness communicates itself. By its very nature as goodness, goodness is always a gift, always shared. Thus, if God is truly good, he desires to and does communicate himself in a beautiful, befitting way that we embodied creatures can understand, a way that marries the spiritual and ineffable to the bodily and comprehensible: incarnation.

This answer about communicability and love may feel a little

---

7. *ST III*.1.1.corp.

ironic, given that this answer comes in a difficult, not-highly-communicable form: Aquinas's technical Latin vocabulary. Words like *essence, nature,* and *fitting* all have specific, formal meanings an untrained reader will miss. Keep in mind that Aquinas has already, earlier in the *Summa,* discussed these words and many others, like *goodness* and *reason,* in argument with other past and present authorities, so we are only getting a snapshot of a much larger and more elaborate conversation.

This technical vocabulary may make readers feel like the scholastic theologians were deliberately excluding people. There's always some vociferous strain of theologians past and present who believe exclusion is a necessary part of the work of theology, whether that's exclusion of women, minority populations, or lay-folk. But in this case, we must be careful to distinguish results from intentions. The scholastics believed that sharing a common and precise vocabulary enabled participants to debate on even ground in their mutual truth-seeking. Reading the *Summa* is more like reading a scientific journal for specialists in behavioral psychology or ornithology than picking up a copy of a more approachable theological text, like Saint Augustine's *Confessions.*[8] The precision in language invites argument and adaptation from the community of scholar-theologians, and there's a world of debate behind each technical term.[9] The Word merits from us not only an emotional response or unthinking devotion, but whole-minded intellectual engagement guided by teachers and wise ones.

---

8. Aquinas even categorizes theology as a *scientia*: a body of knowledge pursued through human reason, limited though such reason may ultimately be. See Frederick Christian Bauerschmidt, *Thomas Aquinas: Faith, Reason, and Following Christ* (Oxford: Oxford University Press, 2013), especially ch. 2.

9. Aquinas, in his highly structured vocabulary, cultivates "a vulnerability to refutation to which one is open simply as a result of being clear enough to be seen, if wrong, to be wrong." Turner, *Aquinas,* 40.

However, we have missed something important by jumping straight to Aquinas's answer. What came *before* this answer? Aquinas begins with objections and questions before getting to his actual argument! Let's go through his method from the beginning as if we were his students learning his style of inquiry.

Step one: Ask the question. Aquinas's first question in this section is "Whether it was fitting that God should become incarnate?" Aquinas's questions are many—they make up the entirety of the *Summa*.

Step two: Introduce potential answers and arguments that disagree with what you're eventually going to argue. To begin with the question and the objections, rather than arguing from what one knows or believes, is an act of faith and trust. These potential oppositions often include quotes from influential church fathers, like Augustine, or from esteemed pagan authorities, like Cicero, Plato, or Aristotle. They present real challenges to his argument. These aren't obviously wrong or foolish answers he can then crush to smithereens, as we might see in a cheap political speech or op-ed today. Rather, they are often shockingly difficult. Here's the first objection that it was not fitting for God to become incarnate, in opposition to Aquinas's own judgment:

> Since God from all eternity is the very essence of goodness, it was best for Him to be as He had been from all eternity. But from all eternity He had been without flesh. Therefore it was most fitting for Him not to be united to flesh.[10]

If God has always been so eternally good and unchanging in that eternal goodness, why did he become united to us in our bodies?

---

10. *ST III*.1.obj.1.

Doesn't that imply something was missing or wrong? It is exactly the same kind of issue that a bright kid brings up to a parent in the car, the kind that leaves you sputtering something dumb because you have never taken that idea seriously enough (or *dared* to take it seriously enough) to question it. Aquinas is relentlessly probing, unafraid to ask the subtle and the obvious, the logical and the creative questions that are difficult to answer even as he is about to argue something different. Everyone knows that we win arguments best if we *don't* engage the strongest objections, if we reverse cherry-pick and cast aside the best parts of opposing arguments to engage with the weakest. Aquinas reminds us that if we are seeking truth in ourselves and our communities, it's not enough to pounce on weakness.

Step three: Answer the question with what you think is the best answer. Now, at last, sometimes pages later, Aquinas answers the initial query with what he thinks is the best answer available. This argument is sometimes quite brief, sometimes multiple paragraphs, depending on the question. In the case of this particular question, this is the answer we first looked at above. But he's not done yet.

Step four: Answer the specific issues raised by the initial answers with which you disagree. It is time to engage directly with the biggest challenges to one's own conclusions, with the insistent question piped from the back seat, or the theological heavyweight nine centuries before your time, or your contemporary who's raising pressing objections in the spirit of your own age. Your own answer is never finished until you have responded to these best other arguments.

This style of argument, back-and-forth questions and answers with past and present community in textual conversation, is called dialectic.[11] Dialectic argument is central to Thomas

---

11. An excellent primer to dialectic is the YouTube video, "Argument and Dialectic (Aquinas 101)," The Thomistic Institute, September 30, 2019, 4:36, https://www.youtube.com/watch?v=RY9vokziX3I.

Aquinas's commitment to communal pursuit of truth. Dialectic is open-ended; while you arrive at a "best" answer, it also means that perhaps another, even better answer may emerge through your mutual rational conversation, even years later. The task of learning how to speak truth about the Word is profoundly communal and humble. Aquinas engages in dialectic because it is flexible, open-ended, an invitation to mutual truth-seeking, a prelude to changing one's mind. He never forgets that debates are an exercise in pride if one is not seeking truth as ardently as one wants one's argument partner to change their mind.

The gift of dialectic like Aquinas's is a theology both structured and free to discuss a strange, wide array of queries about Jesus: questions influenced by Scripture, by the church fathers, by pagan authorities, and by contemporary Aristotelian scholars from the Muslim world like Ibn Sina (Avicenna) and Ibn Rushd (Averroes). Whether it was fitting that Christ prayed for himself?[12] Whether there was wonder, or ignorance, in Christ?[13] Aquinas's Jesus is a Word communicable and explorable through human words, though they cannot fully encompass him.

We begin to see how the shape and form of Thomas Aquinas's God-talk matters deeply because form is the vehicle for the content to be understood in its fullness.

Parables and Scholasticism

In Aquinas's scholastic questions, I am surprisingly reminded of the way Christ himself taught. Yet Jesus's parables and scholasticism are so different from one another! In fact, most

---

12. *ST III*.21.3.
13. *ST III*.15.8, III.15.3.

university-taught theology of any age bears little resemblance to Christ's picture stories of sheep, food, coins, and fathers and sons. What about Thomas Aquinas's obscure, technical theology evokes the parables of Jesus? Eugene Peterson wrote of Christ's favorite and often oblique form of conveying truth, "The parable is a form of speech that has a style all its own. It is a way of saying something that requires the imaginative participation of the listener. Inconspicuously, even surreptitiously, a parable involves the hearer. . . . We ask questions, we think, we imagine."[14]

As in the *Summa*, we meet the Jesus big enough for questions; for argument; for ongoing, shifting interpretation; and for communal imagination. Peterson is not exaggerating. I recently read the gospel of John with a group of friends. In John, Jesus's followers are constantly confused, continually asking questions, always a step or two behind. It made us all laugh. Christ begins conversations with stories meant to provoke questions. Christ invites even the hardest, weirdest questions, especially those that emerge curiously and humbly from acknowledgment of what we do not know. Jesus's storytelling wondrously and strangely opens up new channels of communication and truth-seeking. God-talk, theology that follows the example of Jesus himself, is invitational, communal, and questioning by virtue of its form.

As Aquinas teaches, the incarnation itself is supremely befitting because Christ wonderfully and exactly communicates the goodness, truth, and love of God. The incarnation itself is the marriage of the content of God's Word and the form of the human vessel in which it arrives. As Harvard theologian Mark Jordan has pointed out, Aquinas is confident that every word and act

---

14. Eugene Peterson, *Tell It Slant: A Conversation on the Language of Jesus in His Stories and Prayers* (Grand Rapids: Eerdmans, 2008), 19.

of Christ is meant for our learning. Aquinas quotes a traditional phrase: "Christ's every action is our instruction."[15] When the Word takes on flesh, he "translates" himself, speaks in a manner that we can participate in, follow, and worship, and so begin to distantly understand the love of God and one another. God did not have to reveal himself the way he did, through the embodiment of the divine in Jesus. He could have handed down truth from on high in a thick car owners' manual. It would have been a lot more direct and included more explicit instructions and maybe some helpful diagrams. But the Word Incarnate is the embodied form of God's love.[16]

The Word of God become flesh—Jesus Christ in the incarnation—speaks to us more lovingly and perfectly of God's love than a divine car owner's manual ever could, despite its extreme clarity. Christ himself, as the Word made flesh, is the perfect marriage of form and content. The salvific Word comes to us speaking and dying like us to communicate divine love.

Interpreting and Sharing the Word

Why is the Word uniquely communicable in the incarnation? God created humans as embodied, limited, with finite resources of understanding, what Aquinas following Aristotle called "rational animals."[17] We are incapable of fully understanding the spiritual,

---

15. Mark D. Jordan, *Teaching Bodies: Moral Formation in the Summa of Thomas Aquinas* (New York: Fordham University Press, 2017), 36.

16. John 14:9.

17. See Alasdair MacIntyre, *Dependent Rational Animals: Why Human Beings Need the Virtues* (Chicago: Open Court, 1999) for a wonderful discussion of the relationship between our dependent animal bodies and our rationality shaped by Aquinas's correction of Aristotle.

unseen mysteries of God in our present, embodied life by virtue of our fully good creation as limited creatures. Our own sin and ignorance further impede us. The incarnation is "fitting" not only for God in his goodness but for us as embodied souls.[18]

As embodied souls, we do not learn in isolation; we learn together, from one another, in our present places and bodies—hence, Aquinas's habit of constantly citing other Christians throughout history (in this section, the theologians Pseudo-Dionysius and Augustine of Hippo). Through our eyes and ears, we receive truth and love from reading and listening to one another, and we communicate truth and love back, through our fingers and lips.

Small children put everything in their mouths to discover goodness or badness. As adults our methods become more sophisticated, more funneled through the intellect, yet our senses still guide our reception of truth. The word-packages in which truth arrives matter greatly. We see teachers and holy ones, we hear them, we imitate them. Jesus's embodiment invites us embodied creatures into divine love.

As the church reads and speaks and thinks together about Jesus, revisiting and revising our responses with the great ones of the past and the friends of the present, our intellect works in tandem with our will. Aquinas's dialectic mode of theology reflects a conviction that through working on vocabulary together, through arguing points with one another, through acknowledging those with authority who have learned and studied more than we have, we grow in charity and in communion. We seek Jesus best *together*, and in fact Jesus has created us to seek him this way and delights in it. We laugh, cry, and question as we try to decipher the parables of Jesus alongside

---

18. "Fittingness" loosely translates an important word of Aquinas's, *conveniens* (*ST* III.1.1). Jordan, *Teaching Bodies*, covers this term really helpfully in relation to teaching and moral formation in chs. 1–2.

the disciples. The Word speaks to us in language that we learn together in interpretive community, as he taught the disciples. One of the many identities of the church is the interpretive community of the Word. And in this interpretive community, that Word forms us, and we form one another in love with our words as well.

Like the Word made flesh, our God-talk is married to the words, tones, and contexts in which we speak. Christians have erroneously believed that their message is so important, so central, that the way they convey it no longer matters. The importance of spreading the gospel has been used to justify evils like colonialism and conquest. The Spanish Requirement written in 1510, a declaration of the Spanish monarchy, defended killing indigenous people resisting Spain's conquests in the New World because they were disobeying God's plan to bring the gospel to the Americas.[19] The document itself was read aloud to indigenous people before violently subjugating them, often in Latin without any attempt at explanation whatsoever. Eighteenth- and nineteenth-century theologians like Jonathan Edwards considered the institution of slavery "a means by which to 'civilize' and *evangelize* those in bondage."[20] We can turn our God-talk brutally upon other Christians as well, as Aquinas himself did. In the *Summa* he advocates for the burning of heretics because of their danger to the church and refusal to change their ways.[21] And any user of social media recognizes the cruel God-talk of the online mob. "The ends justify the

---

19. Council of Castile, *Requerimientio 1510*, National Humanities Center Resource Toolbox, accessed February 2023, https://nationalhumanitiescenter.org/pds/amerbegin/contact/text7/requirement.pdf.

20. Kenneth Minkema, "Jonathan Edwards," Yale and Slavery Research Project, accessed February 2023, https://yaleandslavery.yale.edu/jonathan-edwards, emphasis mine.

21. *ST* II.II.11.3.corp. Later, Aquinas's followers, the Dominicans, turned their way with words and emphasis on teaching toward evil in the infamous Spanish Inquisition, which targeted Jews and heretics.

means" is a constant danger for all in the interpretive community of the Word. We have not learned our lesson yet.

Today, shaped by the form of all kinds of media that we consume, people value a provocative argumentative style, from both Christians and non-Christians. What will grab people's dwindling attention spans? As long as they make a splash, who cares if your words answer your opponent's concerns? Too often we praise the equivalent of a blunt axe taken to an argument; the goal is to "own" your opponents, not to persuade them, and especially not to listen to them. Even angelic language without love is less than meaningless, only a gong-like noise (1 Cor. 13:1). In divesting content of form, we are visited with deep irony when the church does try to speak seriously about Jesus. The church's attempts at meaningful, transformative words about Christ become hypocritical hocus pocus—gobbledygook, shorn of meaning, performative.

The *Summa Theologiae* in the logic-driven precision of its language and the immensity of its reach has often been compared to the great gothic cathedrals of medieval Europe, like York Minster or Chartres Cathedral. Every inch of these churches is covered in intricate and sometimes strange interpretation of Scripture and doctrine, via wall paintings, colorful stained glass, and bizarre carvings done by different hands and united by one or more master builders over the years. Paradoxically, the effect is not of a claustrophobic, overcrowded cave, but of light reaching out to light. Cathedrals like York took hundreds of years and many different forms over time in their construction. Great care was taken even in the most obscure corners of the church, and lavish attention to beauty and craftsmanship was cultivated, because this was the home of the Body—the place where bread became the flesh of Christ.

Similarly, the church today must relearn how to take great care with our words. From the casual conversation online to university theology, our words are one of the homes of Jesus, a place where people can meet him, ask questions, and learn how to interpret the Word of God. To avoid hocus pocus about Jesus, we ought to follow Thomas Aquinas at his best and form our God-talk as cathedral-like. Our language takes the worshipful work of years, with attention to correction from others in the diversity of creative perspectives within the human church. In the slow work of words, we rejoice in beauty and truth.

And, of course, both words and cathedrals ever draw the eye toward a yet unreachable light.

Christ beyond Language

Medieval scholasticism's reputation suffered greatly during the Reformation; Protestant and Catholic reformers alike hated the discourse. The famous Catholic humanist Erasmus wished that "scholastic subtleties" "could be thrust into a second place and Christ be taught plainly and simply."[22] As I wrote previously, I wrestled with tracing the value in speaking of things we may never know the answer to, pursuing unanswerable questions together, and especially deciphering a difficult technical vocabulary never found in the Gospels or even at times the creeds.

Yet, all apologies to Erasmus, Christ is never just taught plainly and simply. One does not have to subscribe to scholasticism to recognize that fact. Sure, there are simpler and more complicated ways to teach Jesus, but there's always a human agenda, a human

---

22. In a letter to Capito from James Anthony Froude, *Life and Letters of Erasmus* (United States: C. Scribner's Sons, 1894), 187.

history, *humans* behind God-talk. Not even Christ teaches himself "plainly and simply": read his parables and try to unravel the mystery of Jesus the person. He only gets more mysterious: the mechanics of suffering and the cross, the jubilant resurrection, the end of days. We find ourselves with Aquinas in deep spiritual waters, past the capacities of even the most brilliant men lecturing in a cramped university room in Paris, where our inchoate desire leads us.

While saying Mass at Naples in 1273, Aquinas had a mystical experience. He refused to or could not return to working on the *Summa*. Famously he told a friend that everything he had written now seemed to him "like straw" in comparison to what he had seen.[23] The third part of the *Summa*, the part about Jesus, his body here on earth, and the sacraments he gave his church, Aquinas left unfinished. He died only a few months later, shortly after striking his head on a tree branch on his way to a church council.

At last, Aquinas reminds me of the *tension* at the heart of words about Jesus. We must find ways to speak about Christ together in love; we must also live in the humble knowledge that our creaturely words fall short. We celebrate, follow, and are formed by the words of the learned university theologian; we also acknowledge that in the kingdom of heaven, the holy yet illiterate medieval peasant woman who recites the Our Father in love of her Savior is as faithful and beloved as the theological expert.[24] How

---

23. See Frederick Bauerschmidt, *The Essential Summa Theologiae: A Reader and Commentary*, 2nd ed. (Grand Rapids: Baker Academic, 2021), xxii–xxiii, for a fuller account.

24. Aquinas uses the faith example of the "holy old woman" several times in his exploration of faith. See, for instance, his commentary on the Apostle's Creed, *Expositio in Symbolum Apostolorum*, trans. Joseph B. Collins, ed. Joseph Kenny (New York: 1939), accessed August 2022, https://isidore.co/aquinas/Creed.htm.

we change, shape, and share words matters. Each word falls on ourselves, our friends, and our foes like rain or hail onto tender crops. Those same words are utterly incapable of containing or fully communicating Christ.

We are left with words crumbling in our mouths as the Word Incarnate, perfect marriage of form and content, leads us toward the ineffable, unspeakable face of God.

Meditation and Practices Inspired by the Scholastic Word

- Meditate on the thirteenth chapter of 1 Corinthians. What stands out to you? What kinds of loving practices can you incorporate into your communication with others?

> If I speak in the tongues of humans and of angels but do not have love, I am a noisy gong or a clanging cymbal. And if I have prophetic powers and understand all mysteries and all knowledge and if I have all faith so as to remove mountains but do not have love, I am nothing. If I give away all my possessions and if I hand over my body so that I may boast but do not have love, I gain nothing.
>
> Love is patient; love is kind; love is not envious or boastful or arrogant or rude. It does not insist on its own way; it is not irritable; it keeps no record of wrongs; it does not rejoice in wrongdoing but rejoices in the truth. It bears all things, believes all things, hopes all things, endures all things.
>
> Love never ends. But as for prophecies, they will come to an end; as for tongues, they will cease; as for

knowledge, it will come to an end. For we know only in part, and we prophesy only in part, but when the complete comes, the partial will come to an end. When I was a child, I spoke like a child, I thought like a child, I reasoned like a child. When I became an adult, I put an end to childish ways. For now we see only a reflection, as in a mirror, but then we will see face to face. Now I know only in part; then I will know fully, even as I have been fully known. And now faith, hope, and love remain, these three, and the greatest of these is love.

- For a day, ask questions in conversation whenever you can, rather than immediately offering your opinion or experience. Maybe extend it to a week if you are up for it. See what unfolds and changes in you or your conversations.
- Identify some questions you have been afraid to ask God. Thomas Aquinas's Jesus is big enough for strange questions. There's no need to feel stupid or afraid of seeking truth. If you feel comfortable with it, share these questions with someone you trust and respect, and see what thoughts emerge from your conversation with them.
- If you often speak of Jesus, ask yourself, Am I sharing him in ways fitting to my audience as he himself did?

Prayer

Aquinas composed this prayer to pray before study. I like to pray it before writing or speaking, but it would also fit anytime you need to listen closely.

A Prayer before Study

> *Ineffable Creator,*
>> *Who, from the treasures of Your Wisdom,*
>> *have established three hierarchies of angels,*
>> *have arrayed them in marvelous order*
>>> *above the fiery heavens,*
>> *and have marshaled the regions*
>>> *of the universe with such artful skill,*

> *You are proclaimed*
>> *the true font of light and wisdom,*
>> *and the primal origin*
>>> *raised high beyond all things.*

> *Pour forth a ray of Your brightness*
>> *into the darkened places of my mind;*
>> *disperse from my soul*
>> *the twofold darkness*
>>> *into which I was born:*
>>>> *sin and ignorance.*

> *You make eloquent the tongues of infants.*
> *Refine my speech*
> *and pour forth upon my lips*
> *the goodness of your blessing.*

> *Grant to me*
>> *keenness of mind,*
>> *capacity to remember,*
>> *skill in learning,*

subtlety to interpret,
and eloquence in speech.

May You
guide the beginning of my work,
direct its progress,
and bring it to completion.

You Who are true God and true Man,
Who live and reign, world without end.

Amen.[25]

---

25. Thomas Aquinas, *The Aquinas Prayer Book: The Prayers and Hymns of Thomas Aquinas*, trans. and ed. Robert Anderson and Johann Moser (Manchester, NH: Sophia Institute Press, 2000), 41–43. *The Aquinas Prayer Book* is available for purchase at sophiainstitute.com.

Christ, straight body unbowed by the crucifixion, reminding the viewer that he is still king. Book-cover plaque with Christ on the cross, ivory, ca. 870–880, Walters Art Museum, Baltimore.

The regal lawgiver sits on high, ready to give judgment. *Christ in Majesty*, from the Athelstan Psalter, manuscript illumination, ca. ninth century, Cotton MS Galba A.XVIII fol. 2v, British Library, London.

Public Domain.

Saints and sinners flock below Christ on Judgment Day.
This doomsday imagery prompts reflection from parishioners
also seated below. *The Doom Painting at St. Thomas*, plaster wall
painting, ca. 1470–1500, St. Thomas, Salisbury, Wiltshire, UK.

The graves are emptied, and all come forth to meet Jesus the Judge, whose wounds are visible both as a reminder of what humanity has wrought and of what he has done in love for them. Fra Angelico, *The Last Judgment*, tempera on panel, ca. 1425–1430, Museum of San Marco, Florence.

Alfredo Dagli Orti / Shutterstock.

Christ shows his wounds to the viewer as he comes in justice and mercy. Petrus Christus, *Christ as the Man of Sorrows*, sometimes called *Christ the Savior and Judge*, oil on panel, 1450, Birmingham Museum, Birmingham, UK.

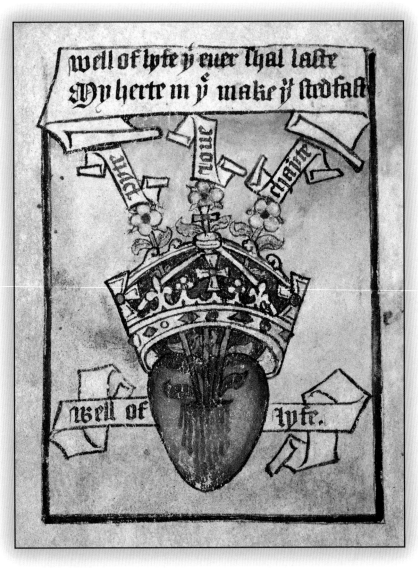

Flowers spring forth from the wounded heart of Jesus, symbols of the fecundity of his love. *Wounded Heart of Christ as the "Well of Lyfe,"* manuscript illumination, ca. 1500, MS Taylor 17, fol. 10v, Princeton University Library, Princeton.

An artistic depiction of Christ's side wound as resembling feminine anatomy. *Christ's Side Wound*, attributed to Jean Le Noir, The Prayer Book of Bonne of Luxembourg, Duchess of Normandy, manuscript illumination, before 1349, fol. 331r, Cloisters Collection, Metropolitan Museum of Art, New York.

Public Domain.

A devoted female lover imitates Christ in bearing a cross as her lover supports and then tenderly undresses her. Christ supports the soul on her cross; Christ tenderly undresses the soul, *Christus unde die minnende Seele*, woodcut, ca. 1460, DG1930/198/6-7, Albertina, Vienna.

Public Domain.

A faithful male lover heeding the summons of Christ to the cross. *Jesus Attracting the Faithful to Heart*, hand-colored woodcut, ca. 1480/1490, 1943.3.853, Rosenwald Collection, National Gallery of Art, Washington, DC. Public Domain.

Jesus gives birth to the church in the agony of his passion. *The Birth of Ecclesia*, manuscript illumination, ca. 1225–1249, ONB Han. Cod. 2554, fol. 2v (detail), Österreichische Nationalbibliothek, Vienna.

Through her prayers, a woman becomes part of the Annunciation alongside the angel Gabriel. *An Owner Present at the Annunciation*, manuscript illumination, ca. 1450–1460, MS 267, fols. 13v–14, Walters Art Museum, Baltimore. Public Domain.

An illustrated scene of the Last Supper emphasizes Eucharistic elements and the priestly calling of Peter. *The Last Supper,* Holkham Bible Picture Book, manuscript illumination, ca. 1327–1335, Add. MS 47682, fol. 28r, British Library, London.

A crowd surrounds Jesus in a semicircle as their bodies and faces reflect different reactions to suffering. Fra Angelico, *The Crucifixion*, tempera on wood, gold ground, ca. 1420–1423, Metropolitan Museum of Art, New York.

Christ's wounds in this crucifixion resemble the skin
ailments suffered by the medieval audience of this altarpiece.
Matthias Grünewald, *The Crucifixion*, Isenheim Altarpiece.
Mixed media (oil and tempera) on limewood panels,
ca. 1512–1516, Musée Unterlinden, Colmar.

Public Domain.

The Father tenderly holds the Son on the cross as the Holy Spirit flutters nearby. Laurent Girardin, *The Trinity*, oil on wood, ca. 1460, Cleveland Museum of Art, Cleveland.

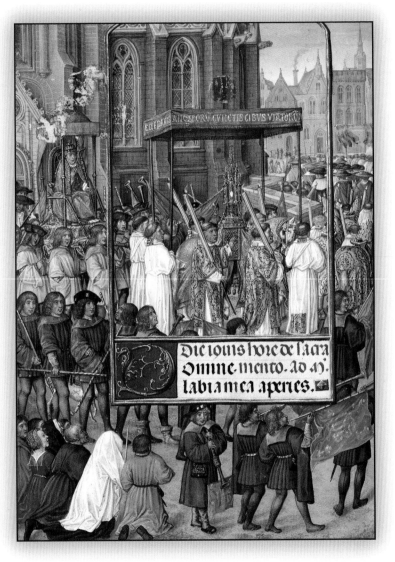

The crowds file out after the Body of Christ on the feast day of Corpus Christi. *Procession for Corpus Christi*, Master of James IV of Scotland, manuscript illumination, ca. 1510–1520, MS Ludwig IX 18 (83.ML.114), fol. 48v, Getty Museum, Los Angeles.

Chapter Six

The Mother

While I was pregnant, my body suddenly drew inordinate attention. At the hardware store and the grocery store, strangers asked me friendly but intrusive questions and touched me without asking. As an introvert, I disliked the attention, well-meaning though it usually was. I became a cultural receptacle of hope I didn't recognize. But at least that was better than being conspicuously ignored. The larger my body grew, the more embarrassing I became in professional spaces. At one academic conference I attended, people pointedly avoided looking at my protruding belly. That avoidance in itself was an awkward and noticeable form of attention. The one time the impending birth was openly acknowledged at that conference was when a well-known scholar cut in front of me, a lowly graduate student, in the line at the refreshments table. She then glanced back, eyes tracing my ungainly silhouette, and quickly stepped behind me, saying, "You need this more than me."

Pregnancy draws attention to embodiment: to inconvenient and even painful present bodies and the strangeness of bodies-in-the-making. Pregnancy invites hope for the future, for new life. It also illustrates our dependence, differences, and weakness. Humans are not autonomous. We did not create ourselves, despite all our efforts to believe the opposite. We are rooted in one another, in the mysteries of belonging to another body and yet becoming ourselves. Yet for all its profundity about our origins, pregnancy is not always glorious. Pregnant women are intimate with pain and new bodily restriction: with morning sickness, increased hunger and exhaustion, stretch marks, and more humiliating features like constipation. To be pregnant is to visibly bear the cumbersome limitations and nascent glory of being embodied. Pregnancy is like the incarnation: glory and hope juxtaposed to the awkward strangeness of the God who created the stars limiting himself to the needy finitude of a baby's body. Jesus labored for our salvation in his embodiment.

Many of us are unfamiliar, even uncomfortable, with the ancient scriptural tradition of Jesus as a mother. This metaphor is not new, New Age, or about Christ's biological sex as a human; it is grounded in robustly theological and biblical metaphor. In fact, themes of labor, pregnancy, and embodiment appear throughout Scripture as an unfolding way of understanding divine, authoritative, and sacrificial love. Paul depicts himself as a mother more often than he describes himself as a father of the newborn churches emerging in the cities of the ancient world.[1] All creation is groaning, laboring, and bringing forth life in Christ (Rom. 8:22). And in the gospels of Matthew and Luke, Jesus describes himself as a mother hen, longing to gather his chicks under his wings (Matt. 23:37; Luke 13:34). Medieval writers latched onto the idea of Jesus as our mother. They developed this image into a full-blown and beautiful theology that helps us to grasp the height and depth of Jesus's love for his children, of Christ's embodiment,

---

1. Beverley Gaventa, *Our Mother Saint Paul* (Louisville: Westminster John Knox, 2007) helpfully explores Pauline imagery of motherhood.

and of his suffering. Pregnancy and labor highlight the scandalous weakness, discomfort, and hidden splendor of the incarnation. Exploring a mother's inexplicably powerful love for such a small and helpless creature as a baby helps us to penetrate the mysteries of divine love.

Misogyny and the Divine Feminine

The translator of what would become the standard Bible of the medieval church, the influential Saint Jerome, placed women and childbirth very low on the spiritual ladder of holiness. In a sour dispatch from the fourth century, he writes, "As long as a woman is for birth and children, she is as different from man as body is from soul.... But when she wishes to serve Christ more than the world, she will cease to be a woman and will be called a man."[2]

Gee thanks, Jerome. I can't wait until I'm spiritually mature enough to be called a man. Sadly, Jerome was not unique. He reflected the views of his misogynistic culture. This belief about the inferiority of women's bodies, spirituality, and mental capacity in comparison to men's was common for the next thousand years and more, although it took varying forms.[3] Throughout the Middle Ages, whole systems of thought were predicated on the bodily, spiritual, and moral subordination of women.

2. Saint Jerome, "Commentarius in Epistolam ad Ephesios 3.5," quoted in Dyan Elliott, "Gender and Christian Traditions," *Oxford Handbook of Women and Gender in Medieval Europe*, ed. Judith M. Bennet and Ruth Mazo Karras (Oxford: Oxford University Press, 2013).

3. Beth Allison Barr has recently written about how the historical church continued cultural, patriarchal traditions of subjugating women, rather than following the far more difficult and controversial path pioneered by Jesus, who elevated and valued women. See Barr, *The Making of Biblical Womanhood: How the Subjugation of Women Became Gospel Truth* (Grand Rapids: Brazos, 2021).

Male theologians wrote volumes on Genesis and the fall of Eve, a narrative they felt showed the moral and spiritual inferiority of women to men. The scientific theories of the time confirmed these convictions. According to Aristotle and his followers, female bodies were deformed male bodies that had failed to develop properly in the womb because they had not received enough warmth, causing their sexual organs to grow inside the body rather than outside.[4]

Monks, too, tended to take a grim view of the value of women: They often saw them through a prism of sexual temptation (a view that has sadly never quite disappeared from Christianity). Women's bodies were sites of sin and a threat to the superior male. But fascinatingly, the medieval popularity of the idea of Jesus as a mother did not originate with women or even laypeople, but with the monastic theologians, as the historian Caroline Walker Bynum has extensively documented.[5] Monks like Bernard of Clairvaux, Aelred of Rievaulx, and Anselm of Canterbury explored facets of compassionate leadership and authority through the figure of Jesus as a mother.[6] Given the systemic prejudice against women that often became simply unveiled hatred, especially against women's bodies, why would monks take up this feminized version of Jesus so enthusiastically?

Despite their misogyny, monks were skilled readers of Scripture. They noticed something we today often do not: God as a father is everywhere in holy Scripture, but the idea of Jesus

---

4. For Aristotle's views on the differences between male and female, see Aristotle, *On the Generation of Animals* (Electronic Scholarly Publishing Project, 2017), PDF accessed August 29, 2021, http://www.esp.org/books/aristotle/generation-of-animals/.

5. Caroline Walker Bynum, *Jesus as Mother: Studies in the Spirituality of the High Middle Ages* (Berkeley: University of California Press, 1982), especially ch. 4, "Jesus as Mother and Abbot as Mother: Some Themes in Twelfth-Century Cistercian Writing."

6. Bynum, *Jesus as Mother*, 154–59.

as a mother is there too. The medieval monk-theologians began to experiment with this image. They noticed how Jesus often did humble tasks usually performed by women in the ancient Middle East, like serving others and washing feet. Jesus pointedly represented himself as a vessel through which people would be "born again," the phrase that baffled Nicodemus in the third chapter of John. Bernard, Anselm, and Aelred began to write of themselves as Jesus-like mothers, suffering in their compassion for the brothers under their authority, filled with the mother's milk of mercy and tender love.[7]

Contemplative writers, often women, and artists of the twelfth, thirteenth, and fourteenth centuries took the image a step further. These writers and artists asked, What would happen if we depicted that image literally? To be born again became more than a mere figure of speech in these images. Remember the images from the "Lover" chapter? Christ's side wound resembled a vulva, as he gave birth to the church. They wrote Jesus as a pregnant, laboring, and postpartum mother: lactating, bleeding, meant to be adored and imitated in his long-suffering mercy and compassion. The crucifixion and childbirth meet at a strange point of willing love and willing suffering in the service of abundant life.

Thinking of Jesus as a laboring mother powerfully contextualizes Jesus's suffering. The crucifixion is not suffering for suffering's sake, as it has sometimes been depicted. Suffering alone is not redemptive, though we often can mistake it as such in our attempts to make sense of the world. Christ's passion is more similar to childbirth than to cancer, wounds received in war, accidental injury, leprosy, COVID-19, or any other bodily affliction.

---

7. See, for instance, Bernard's depiction of himself in his letters, quoted extensively in Bynum, *Jesus as Mother*, 116–17.

Though in his agony Christ encompasses, shares, and knows all other pain, his suffering is profoundly generative, just as in childbirth. He gives birth to us in his passion, his resurrection, and his life of love.

Jesus gives birth to the church in the agony of his passion. *The Birth of Ecclesia*, manuscript illumination, ca. 1225–1249, ONB Han. Cod. 2554, fol. 2v (detail), Österreichische Nationalbibliothek, Vienna.

Perhaps it seems morbid to compare labor to the passion. But for medieval people, this would have been a natural and even comforting idea. For medieval women, birth was a dangerous and often lethal undertaking—one reason why I, as a mother and medie-valist, can get a little irritated when people too heavily empha-size how natural birth is for women. In medieval Florence, one in five women died during labor.[8] Caesarean sections were used only if the mother died but the baby was still alive, because the procedure was a death sentence for the mother.[9] And life was not assured even in the case of a successful, living birth. In the medie-val English village of Wharram Percy, about 20 percent of infants died before they reached the age of two.[10] Every medieval mother-to-be knew she was staring down her possible demise as birth drew closer. And she was keenly aware that her child might breathe only for a brief span. Nowhere was the fragility of the human body so evident as in the process of giving new life. Women writers of the Middle Ages recognized the human frailty, sacrifice, and suffering of birth as a brilliant way into understanding Jesus's salvific labors in his life and on the cross.

Marguerite of Oingt, a twelfth-century Carthusian prioress, characterized Jesus as a laboring mother not just in the moment of the cross but in the course of his whole life:

> Oh, Sweet Lord Jesus Christ, who ever saw any mother suffer such a birth! But when the hour of the birth came you were placed on the hard bed of the cross where you could not move or turn around or stretch your limbs as someone who suffers

8. Elma Brenner, "The Medieval Childbirth Guide: 6 Tips for Pregnant Mothers in the Middle Ages," BBC *History Magazine* (February 2021), https://www.historyex-tra.com/period/medieval/middle-ages-childbirth-dangers-mothers-midwives-how-did-medieval-women-give-birth/.

9. Brenner, "The Medieval Childbirth Guide."

10. Mary E. Lewis and Rebecca Gowland, "Brief and Precarious Lives: Infant Mortality in Contrasting Sites from Medieval and Post-medieval England," *American Journal of Physical Anthropology* 134, no. 1 (September 2007): 117–29, https://doi.org/10.1002/ajpa.20643.

such great pain should be able to do; and seeing this, they stretched you out and fixed you with nails and you were so stretched that there was no bone left that could still have been disjointed, and your nerves and all your veins were broken. And surely it was no wonder that your veins were broken when you gave birth to the world all in one day.[11]

Marguerite visualized a Jesus who underwent the increasing pain of labor throughout his life, as his death drew nearer. Like a medieval mother, he knew that deeper and deeper pain awaited in the process of giving life to his children.

During the medieval period, women did not typically give birth on beds as they do today. In the absence of epidurals and painkillers, midwives encouraged women to pace around the room and eventually squat during the final stages of labor on a birthing stool to manage pain and quicken the process. Gravity, movement, and position aided both infant and mother in the final, most agonizing stretch of birth. In contrast, Marguerite's Jesus is pinned in place on the cross, his body unbearably stretched. He cannot follow the medieval pain-reducing conventions. Marguerite knew that the bodies of human mothers are stretched and burdened further with the more children they carry. Jesus bears and births all of humanity within his agonized, mortal body. Because of his many children, not a single sinew, muscle, or joint of Christ's body is left intact. Crucifixion and birth merge in one image of devastating, sacrificial, maternal love.

What was the point of this image of the agonized Mother Jesus? To increase guilt, obedience, and a sense of indebtedness, like a mother who constantly reminds her wayward teenagers how

---

11. *The Writings of Margaret of Oingt: Medieval Prioress and Mystic*, trans. Renate Blumenfeld-Kosinski (Cambridge: D. S. Brewer, 1990), 31.

much she suffered for them fifteen years prior? Some might have understood it that way, but that was not the point. Nor was it part of some Christian project to glorify motherhood over other forms of femininity—which is actually a misguided and painful legacy of post-Reformation Christianity rather than anything remotely medieval.[12] This suffering Mother Jesus is a fellow traveler with the suffering mothers and women of the Middle Ages. During labor, medieval women usually looked at the cross while they travailed in pain and hope. Jesus on the cross means that one never truly suffers alone. Additionally, and importantly, the image of Jesus as a laboring mother in his passion meant that women's bodies, and women's labors, were redeemed too. Female bodies were no longer only sites of sin. One did not have to inhabit a male body to be fully Christian; a female body fully and fittingly participates in the cocreation and redemption of humanity.

Jesus Our Mother Loves Us in Our Bodies

The fourteenth-century writer Julian of Norwich explores this feminine, embodied love of Jesus at length in her wonderful *Revelations of Divine Love*. At the age of thirty, amid a life-threatening illness, Julian received a series of what she called "showings," sights and sounds from God. This experience led her to become an anchorite, walled into the side of a medieval church. Living in a tiny cell, with one window to the outside world and one window into the church so she could participate in the liturgy

---

12. See chapter 4, "The Cost of the Reformation for Evangelical Women," in Barr, *The Making of Biblical Womanhood*.

and life of the parish, Julian read and meditated, prayed and composed. She would think on her visionary experience for the rest of her life, eventually composing her showings into a book for her "evencristen," her brothers and sisters in Jesus.

For Julian, Jesus's maternity was not just a nice metaphor, his love and pain in childbirth meant to move us. It expressed something essential to Jesus. She understood the love of a mother as the most helpful paradigm for us to begin to understand how deep is Jesus's love, and how wide, how strong, and how close. Julian wrote that Christ himself does the "service" and "office" of motherhood in all things. This office only he can fulfill in love's entirety: "The mother's service is nearest, readiest, and surest: nearest because it is most natural, readiest because it is most loving, and surest because it is truest. No one ever might or could perform this office fully, except only him."[13] So it is not that motherhood on earth, our own mothers, or you yourself if you are a mother are a model to help us understand Christ's mothering. Christ's mothering is the original and only truly full mothering, childbearing, and child raising.

One may bristle a bit at Julian's assumption that fathers are less close, ready, and merciful in their parenting than mothers. Yet parenting has cultural norms as well as biological differences. In the fourteenth century, fathers certainly were associated with paternal love, discipline, and especially protection of their children, but not with the day-to-day tasks of caring intimately for a child's physical and emotional needs. Fathers did not typically change diapers, dress their children, feed them, or carry them about as they did household tasks. Mothers suffered the pangs

---

13. *The Writings of Julian of Norwich: A Vision Showed to a Devout Woman and A Revelation of Love*, ed. Nicholas Watson and Jacqueline Jenkins (University Park: Pennsylvania State University Press, 2006), 60.12–14. Lightly translated by myself for easier reading.

of breastfeeding, woke in the night, and washed filthy swaddling clothes in the age before disposable diapers. Some mothers carried their children to the field, their babies wrapped tightly on their backs as they brought in the harvest. Fathers could come and go for days at a time, and did so often. Loving fathers went about the daily business of life: traveling on market days, going to war, working in the fields and forges, castles and ships. But the life of an infant was dependent on the physical presence and tender, attentive closeness of her mother. Motherhood entailed a different kind of love connected to physical presence and intimacy.

Julian wrote in chapter 60 of the Long Text of her *Showings*, "Our great God, the supreme wisdom of all things, arrayed and prepared himself in this humble place [Mary's womb], all ready in our poor flesh, himself to do the service and the office of motherhood in everything."[14] Julian envisaged the moment of the incarnation and redemption as a womb within a womb, birth upon birth. Mary carries Christ, who carries the world as the ultimate mother. Christ's motherhood is incarnational; it is about embodiment, the formation of bodies, and the community and love that come with bodies specifically.

This embodiment-based love is not just a memory of the distant past of pregnancy, labor, and nursing. It belongs to those who intimately and compassionately care for the day-to-day minute, embodied needs of a young child as they grow familiar with all that child's particularities, the historical role in parenting long played by mothers. I had not expected to be so in love with the specific physical details of my children: the perfect curve of my eldest's nose in profile, the impossibly large, anime-character eyes of my middle. My youngest, Constance, is almost a year and a half

14. *Writings of Julian of Norwich*, 60.9–11.

as I write this. She loves hats, especially crowns (we call her the Baby Queen). She is also obsessed with shoes and socks and insists on wearing her shoes all day long. Her legs in this warm end-of-summer season are usually bare. They are stocky and strong; they descend in straight lines, with no discernable ankles, into her beloved tiny shoes. Those fat baby legs are heavenly. My love for the Baby Queen is inextricable from her embodiment and from my own. Christ loves like a mother, his love inseparable from our funny particularities, like I love Constance. Jesus adores our created bodies, the way our legs, noses, and eyes are shaped, how we love hats or writing or rock climbing.

Yet as Julian reminds us, this intimate, embodied love of Jesus our Mother does not come from our merits or the beauty of our bodies. We have often been told implicitly or explicitly that we need to be a certain way to be worthy of love, often by our human parents as we grew up. I'm sure I communicate that message to my children at times. But Constance did not earn my love through her delightful baby legs. She came into the world from myself, in my pain and cocreation, and I loved her. Paradoxically, my children belong to themselves entirely as well. Each of them emerged as their own person. They are not mere reflections of my husband or myself, or blank canvases on which to project my dreams and hopes. And I love that about them, though sometimes when I get frightened, tired, or self-absorbed, I forget and try to possess them or make them more understandable copies of myself.

God sees us and loves us, Julian insisted, in the bodies we often disparage or neglect, in our passions and acts and thoughts. Unlike me, the earthly mother, he loves that way perfectly, without the stain of possessiveness, selfishness, or fear. My love for my children is a singing echo of Christ the Mother's perfect love for us. He belongs to us in the bodily, day-to-day intimacy distinctive to mothers and very young children. And we belong to him in our bodies; we are born spiritually and literally through the Son in his role as cocreator.[15] Paradoxically, we are in him while also our own.

Mother Jesus and Suffering

Does such powerful love—love of who we truly are and not of our potential, talents, or beauty—change how we respond in our pain and suffering to Jesus and to one another? Should it change how we envision ourselves and our way of being in the world? Julian thought so. She described Jesus as mothering from pregnancy through childhood, kindling our understanding, preparing our ways, easing our consciences, and comforting our souls: "And he makes us to love all that he loves for the sake of his love, and to be well satisfied with him and all his works. And when we fall, hastily he raises us with his lovely calling and gracious touch."[16] This beautiful passage suggests a divine version of a profoundly human practice of mothering. My heart never swells so much as when my oldest daughter learns to love something I find lovely, from flowers to stories to people. Her love for daffodils will never cease to bring me joy. The small, tender shoots of compassion and justice growing in her heart's soil can move me to tears. But Julian's primary concern was with that last sentence: What happens when we, the children of God, fall?

Falling is a usefully ambiguous word. It can encompass something as simple as tripping and sprawling flat on your face, or it can refer to bodily illness. Falling can also reference *the* fall,

<hr>

15. The Son takes a unique role in creation. Cf. John 1:3, 10; Colossians 1:16; Hebrews 1:2.

16. *Writings of Julian of Norwich*, 61.3–8.

the great and repeated rejection of our creation and embodiedness in our aims to be the masters of the universe. That can include our dozens of small failures, intentional or unintentional, throughout an ordinary day: ignoring a needy child, driving rudely, snapping at our spouse. We fall all the time, just like a child learning how to walk. But we all hate falling or, at the very least, recognizing our falls.

Yet Julian insisted that falling is necessary in this life:

> He allows some of us to fall more hard and more grievously than we ever did before, as we think. And then we, who are so often unwise, believe that everything we have done is nothing, wasted. But it is not so. We need to fall, and we need to see our falling.
>
> For if we did not fall, we would not know how frail and wretched we are on our own, nor would we know as fully the marvelous love of our maker. . . . Nevertheless, we shall truly see that we were never damaged in God's love, nor were we the less of price in his sight. . . . For hard and marvelous is that love which may not, nor will not, be broken from trespass.[17]

We must witness our own failures, sin, mistakes, and need for others. Otherwise, the temptation to think ourselves more autonomous and more powerful than we really are is too great.

To cast this situation back into a parenting example helps it to make sense. Children learn about the world and themselves through their falls. They learn they are mortal, made of flesh and bone and not invincible. They discover that they need other people. They learn to share by failing to share and then trying

---

17. *Writings of Julian of Norwich*, 61.12–22.

again, or by wishing to be shared with when their playmate isn't sharing. An attentive parent is constantly navigating where to intervene in a child's falls. While an incapable swimmer falling into a pool is bad, curiously sticking one's face underwater then coughing up some water is good. There's no other way for a small child to discover the profound limitations of their human lungs. Through small falls, a child learns to trust her parents' judgment. Parents may know something she does not know. Julian's argument about falling is similar. Falling, even in sin, helps us to understand how we as humans need our Mother and need one another. Our failures reveal to us the necessity of community, of care, and of healthy respect for our physical and mental limitations.

Julian still believed sin was evil and that its consequences were grave. She wasn't living in a fantasy world in her little cell at St. Julian's in Norwich. Like us, she lived in a time rife with political and religious corruption, besieged by terrible pandemics, drowning in prejudice, seething with ignorance and violence. But she argued that Jesus loves his child even when that child does something horrible: his love is "hard and marvelous," for no trespass can break it.

While the pain and truth of falling are real, Julian believed the deeper problem was that after we fall, we flee or deny our Mother, our falls, and their consequences. Hiding, fleeing, acting out, constructing new narratives to cast oneself in the best light, making apologies that aren't admissions of guilt or apologies at all, blaming other people for one's own mistakes or failures—these are common responses to falls of all kinds. I am pretty good at all of these things—most of us are. We, the children of Jesus, often avoid our failures to the extent that we avoid learning from them or anything that follows. This is how sin becomes protected and even cherished in our behavior, even in our social systems. It's how personal relationships can remain broken over relatively minor issues. It's also, to overly simplify complex problems, how sexism becomes installed in churches as doctrinal or how racism builds into judicial systems as tradition enshrined in law.

Julian urgently wanted her readers to know that if Jesus indeed loves like a mother—the most natural, compassionate, loving mother—then much of how we have approached him in and after our falls is wrong. Christians often act like teenagers lying and then acting out, or toddlers pooping behind the couch thinking their mistake is well-hidden, or even just kids trying to be good because they're terrified that one misstep will trigger an incomprehensible wrath. We do not need to fear such things, Julian argued. Instead, we must acknowledge our need for our Mother and for one another in our malice, errors, and embodied frailty.

> Our courteous mother does not will that we flee away— nothing could be less desirable to him. He wills that we take on the condition of a child. For when a child is discomfited, diseased, or afraid, she runs hastily to her mother. And if she cannot run, she cries upon her mother for help with all her might. So Christ wills that we do as the humble child, saying thus: "My kind mother, my gracious mother, my dearest mother, have mercy on me. I have made myself foul and dissimilar to you, and I cannot fix it myself, only with your help and grace." And even if we don't feel easily comforted in our calling out, we can trust that Jesus always takes on the condition of a wise mother.[18]

---

18. *Writings of Julian of Norwich*, 61.36–43.

This is a scene of confession, the opposite of defiance, defensiveness, or fleeing. Confession requires both the painful acknowledgment of our mistakes, stupidity, sin, and limitations, as well as trust that in that moment of vulnerability someone is waiting and listening in love.

This passage can also be difficult to work through because it involves two issues combined under the banner of suffering: willful sin and accidental pain. Julian conflates them because they are both falling and they both prompt humans to recognize our limitations and trust our Mother. Because of this ambiguity in falling, this description of Julian's and the quiet will of Christ our Mother that we trust him in our falls may also make one angry, uncomfortable, or resistant. Some of us have gone through horrible pain inflicted by others or by ourselves. Some of us have had inexplicably terrible things happen to us without real rhyme or reason: childhood trauma, terminal diagnoses, abuse. *Why?* We want reasons; we want explanations that make all the bad things worth it in our eyes. Malcolm Gladwell, in an interview with Professor Kate Bowler, stated, "We have, as human beings, a storytelling problem. We're a bit too quick to come up with explanations for things we don't really have an explanation for."[19] Kate Bowler, who received all kinds of reasons for her suffering from well-meaning folks after a terminal cancer diagnosis, calls these "the lies we love."[20] Julian of Norwich looked squarely and bravely at the fact that in many of our falls, we just will not understand why.

---

19. Kate Bowler, interview with Malcolm Gladwell, "Malcom Gladwell: Can People Change?," *Everything Happens with Kate Bowler*, podcast, August 17, 2021, https://podcasts .apple .com /us /podcast /malcolm -gladwell -can -people -change /id1341076079?i=1000532230901.

20. Kate Bowler, *Everything Happens for a Reason and Other Lies I've Loved* (New York: Random House, 2018).

Julian did not try to "justify the ways of God to man," as John Milton would attempt to do two hundred years later in his epic *Paradise Lost*. She used a familiar picture, a mother loving a child, to help us enter into twin discomfort and truth: we are limited children, often suffering for reasons we do not understand, and Jesus is an attentive mother who loves us as our whole selves. *God loves us, and our falls hurt badly.* These truths coexist, sometimes in the splendor of good in the face of evil, and sometimes only in pain, exhaustion, and sadness.

At the age of two, my oldest daughter, Margaret, had an asthma attack in the midst of a minor cold. I took her wearily to the pediatrician, which she already hated and feared. The oxygen in her blood was low, so she had to receive breathing treatments. This was the first time she ever needed them, and she fought the mask on her face with every ounce of her toddler strength. In vain, I put the mask on her beloved stuffed Pink Bunny to make it easier. I screened the doctor's office episode of *Daniel Tiger* for her on my phone. I put the mask on myself. I sang, I explained, I cajoled, I offered rewards in vain. She screamed in furious fear every time the oxygen mask approached her face, which did not help the asthma attack. It all ended with me forcibly holding the mask to her face for three hours as she raged and screamed in my stiff, unyielding arms, the happy music of *Daniel Tiger* and my words blending into her wails until she finally, listlessly gave up her battle and fell against me, not with trust but with exhaustion and despair. No amount of reasoning would have made it better.

I understand it from her perspective. If I love her, as I claim, why would I bring her to a place she did not like? Why did I coldly hold her down and force the mask on her tiny, terrified face? I was trusted and beloved, and I betrayed her. She already couldn't breathe well, and to hold that oxygen mask on her face felt like precisely the wrong thing to do. In the end she went home; what was the point of that wretched interlude in the cheerless pediatrician's office? She knew nothing of blood oxygen levels or of looming trips to the ER. We went home from the pediatrician's office, Margaret's blood oxygen levels at last steady and normal. I sobbed in the car.

It was a small moment in one tiny life. People have certainly faced more devastating and true terrors than Margaret and her oxygen mask. But to a two-year-old it felt as nightmarish as anything could. I'm not God (hooray), and to this day when I think about that episode, I wish it had gone differently. But as the parent, with a longer-reaching perspective, with knowledge about oxygen and blood and asthma, with care and compassion and love for my child, I made that decision. And thankfully, Margaret made the decision to trust me again and again and again because of her childhood and my motherhood. It took a few days of her side-eyeing me and pointedly preferring her dad. Our Mother's love is hard and marvelous. So is a child's trust.

In some ways, this story—and the whole image of Christ as a mother and we as his children—is the closest analogue I can find to an adequate theodicy. And yet it isn't enough. It does not make sense of the pandemic. It cannot reason through the tragedy of a friend who died of cancer before the age of thirty, leaving his young family to live without him. It won't explain the devastation of Afghanistan. That's the tip of the iceberg of hard things I have no words for.

The only thing to do is to admit that I just do not understand, like a young child, and then run to Christ's mothering love, his very essence. Faced with our limitations, our need for one another, and our need for our Mother, I am learning how to embrace my lack in my embodiment. Like my daughter-teacher Margaret,

I learn to trust—though sometimes that trust means just acknowledging my fear and exhaustion and utter lack of control.

Mother Jesus is present to us, as a mother is present to her children. He tells us he loves us as a faithful mother loves her baby: with a special attachment to the joy and absurdity of our minds and our bodies; with a special attention to the neediness embedded in those wonderful, limited bodies and minds; with a special compassion and mercy in our suffering. Julian's Mother Jesus reminds us that we are still growing up.

Meditation and Practices Inspired by Jesus Our Mother

- Meditate on Matthew 23:37. What stands out to you? In what ways have you been hiding or running from Mother Jesus, who longs to gather you under his wings?

  > "Jerusalem, Jerusalem, the city that kills the prophets and stones those who are sent to it! How often have I desired to gather your children together as a hen gathers her brood under her wings, and you were not willing!"

- Think back on a distinct moment in your childhood when you felt seen, loved, and known by an adult who cared for you—parent, teacher, guardian, grandparent, family friend. Write it down if it helps you, or tell a friend. Try to recall the specific feeling of being known, loved, and protected in your particularity, your unique and created self. In this practice, catch a glimpse of the way Christ loves you, not just as a depersonalized soul but as an embodied, created child of God.

- Where do you need to embrace your dependence and smallness as a child? Find a warm, cozy place, like a bed or a couch with a blanket. Or find a place that makes you feel physically small, like underneath the vast sky at night. Lean into your identity as a beloved, created, limited child as you identify and confess your limitations, sins, or errors before your mother Jesus. Confess especially things you do not understand but have been trying to control.

Prayer

Anselm of Canterbury (1033–1109), Cistercian abbot and archbishop of Canterbury in the twelfth century, provides us with a prayer for this chapter:

Christ, mother, who gathers under your wings your little ones, your dead chick seeks refuge under your wings. For by your gentleness, those who are hurt are comforted; by your perfume, the despairing are reformed. Your warmth resuscitates the dead; your touch justifies sinners. . . . Console your chicken, resuscitate your dead one, justify your sinner. May your injured one be consoled by you; may he or she who of his or herself despairs be comforted by you and reformed through you in your complete and unceasing grace. For the consolation of the wretched flows from you, blessed, world without end. Amen.[21]

---

21. Saint Anselm of Canterbury, "Prayer 10 to Christ and St. Paul," quoted from Bynum, *Jesus as Mother*, 114–15.

Chapter Seven

The Good Medieval Christian

One of my favorite medieval pieces of art is a two-page spread of the Annunciation, the moment the angel Gabriel came to Mary. It's from an elaborate fifteenth-century book of hours, a prayer book that adapted the monastic cycle of liturgy and Scripture for layfolk. On the left, the angel Gabriel bows his head reverently, proclaiming: *Ave Maria, gratia plena* [Hail Mary, full of grace]*!* On the right, medievally dressed Mary has been caught in the act of prayer; she turns her head toward the divine messenger. The dove descends, sent by God the Father from a miniature window into heaven. But the part that tickles me is that Gabriel is not alone on his side. He stands behind a laywoman, the owner of the manuscript, also dressed in her medieval best (wearing the infamous pointy cone hat of princess Halloween costumes today). *She* faces Mary, partially obscuring the archangel. She kneels in prayer yet is physically present at the consummation of history, the very first arrival of the Christ. Gabriel even has his hand on this woman's shoulder—as if they are announcing the Messiah's imminent arrival together!

An Owner Present at the Annunciation, manuscript illumination, ca. 1450–1460, MS 267, fols. 13v–14, Walters Art Museum, Baltimore.
Public Domain.

I experience a strange blend of feelings and thoughts while meditating on this art. My first, rather puritanical thought: "How could she have herself painted into the moment of creation's rebirth? How arrogant!" But then my second: "I want to be there too!" Her hope is bold-faced on the prayer book page, a hope we share. She wants to become present, witness to the risen Christ in all moments of history. She does so by entering into his life through reading and prayer, so deeply that she becomes a participant in salvation history.

Patrons or owners regularly hired medieval artists to insert them into scriptural or saintly narratives in these breathtaking books of hours, also sometimes called the little hours, *horae*, or hours of the Virgin.[1] The lavish books were often status symbols, painted with gold leaf and rare, glimmering inks at a time when all books were handmade luxury items. Eustache Deschamps, the popular fourteenth-century French poet, even wrote a sarcastic ditty about them in which he skewered the tendency of the wealthy to show off their prayer books.[2] In the classic paradoxes of every age of Christianity, these prayer books were costly bespoke objects for showing off *and* a way into a meditative communion with Jesus, the God who shared our humanity.

A profound theology is at work in the humanity they display. Even in all our silliness and desire to show off, the lady with Gabriel reminds us that we too belong to salvation history. Any gap between gold-leafed life in church on Sunday and humdrum life during the week is artificial. The Annunciation is part of shared human history, the one with crying babies, jobs you don't enjoy, your favorite restaurant, all of it. I'm human. Jesus is human. This is the wellspring of hope.

This prayer book encapsulates another tension we live in as followers of Jesus. When the Word became flesh, he became more like us and we were freed to become more like him. Often we do become more like him, in the slow unfolding of grace, long development of virtue, and hard-earned lessons on being wholly human. Equally often, however, we refashion him in *our* image. Frequently we aren't even aware of the difference. We genuinely adore him. We place him in gorgeous prayer books that help us

---

1. See Eamon Duffy's beautiful book *Marking the Hours: English People and Their Prayers 1240–1570* (New Haven: Yale University Press, 2006) for an illustrated exploration of *horae*.
2. Find a translated version of this funny ditty in Duffy, *Marking the Hours*, 21.

to show off both our wealth and devotion (in more contemporary parlance, "#blessed"). We worship him; then we virtue signal or use him as a tool to further our cause. This chapter is about the human Jesus, both the gracious incarnate God who speaks to us exactly where we are and the god we make in our image.

The book we are about to dive into is entitled *The Mirror of the Blessed Life of Jesus Christ*, by the Carthusian prior (head monk of his monastery) Nicholas Love. In the Middle Ages, mirror (Latin *speculum*) literature was encyclopedic, reflecting the world around readers clearly back to them.[3] And like a mirror, these prayer books and the whole sweep of imaginative devotion to the human Jesus both reveal the image of God and reflect our own faces back to ourselves.

A Medieval Bestseller

Far from being a monolith, the Middle Ages, like today, had factions, fads, and fluctuations in religion and devotion.[4] As people read more in private, there was a huge upswell of interest in devotional texts in fourteenth-century Europe. In England, more books were written: books of hours, works of contemplative theology from authors like Julian of Norwich and Walter Hilton, and penitential texts, which helped medieval readers prepare for confession through identifying their sins and cultivating contrition—all to aid devotional practices outside and inside churches and monasteries. Many of these genres had long existed in Latin versions,

---

3. Ritamary Bradley, "Backgrounds of the Title *Speculum* in Mediaeval Literature," *Speculum* 29, no. 1 (January 1954): 100–115, https://doi.org/10.2307/2853870.

4. For a snapshot of Nicholas Love's age, see John Van Engen, "Multiple Options: The World of the Fifteenth-Century Church," *Church History* 77, no. 2 (June 2008): 257–84, https://doi.org/10.1017/S0009640708000541.

but their English translation was a new development. One particularly flourishing tradition encouraged deep, personal relationship with Jesus based on envisioning the events of the Gospels. This imaginative, guided activity was meant to uncover Christ's love and cultivate one's love for Christ in return. Nicholas Love called this process "devout imagination."[5]

His book is an adaptation and translation of one of the most influential and popular books of the late medieval era, the Latin *Meditationes Vitae Christi*, or *Meditations on the Life of Christ*. *Meditationes* is a retelling of the Gospels with some extrabiblical material, like narratives of Mary's childhood and theological reflections from major theologians like Bernard of Clairvaux and Augustine of Hippo. It was likely composed by a fourteenth-century Franciscan friar or nun who lived among the glorious towers of San Gimignano, Italy.[6]

While *Meditationes* was never intended to replace Scripture, it aimed to increase one's love for God by portraying the life of Christ and the sacraments of the church in such a way that regular medieval folks—those who were not monks, nuns, or priests—could meditate on gospel and sacraments in a spiritually transformative, *personal* exercise.

Meditationes was so popular that it was translated over and over into local European languages: dialects of medieval Germany, France, and Spain, as well as English, Dutch, Gaelic,

---

5. Nicholas Love, *The Mirror of the Blessed Life of Jesus Christ: A Full Critical Edition*, ed. Michael G. Sargent (New York: Routledge, 2018), 10. I have lightly translated all Middle English quotations from *Mirror* into modern English.

6. Sargent, in the introduction to *Mirror*, thoroughly covers cultural contexts and versions. Sarah McNamer has recently proposed the author was a nun rather than a monk, but not everyone agrees. See the introduction to *Meditations on the Life of Christ: The Short Italian Text*, ed. Sarah McNamer (Notre Dame, IN: University of Notre Dame Press, 2018).

Swedish, Bulgarian, and more.[7] One popular adaptation was by Saint Ludolph of Saxony, whose version would be printed eighty-eight times in seven languages in the two centuries after its composition.[8] One of those translations would later be read to a convalescent Ignatius of Loyola, influencing the future saint's "spiritual exercises" and igniting a spirituality that powerfully forms Christians to the present day.[9] Nicholas Love's *Mirror of the Blessed Life of Jesus Christ* was the most popular English version.

Love's *Mirror* retold scenes from Scripture in English as spiritual food for "simple" souls, meaning those Christians, especially women, untrained in theology.[10] Mediated by Love's clerical authority and sanctioned by the hierarchy of the medieval church, *Mirror* narrates the life and death of Jesus. Despite the "simple souls" remark, it's not exactly watered down. Love carefully describes difficult concepts like Trinitarian doctrine. He intentionally focuses on the bodily, human life of Christ to "stir" and "ravish" the ordinary person into recognizing and desiring the invisible spiritual life.[11] Such a practice, he notes, stabilizes the heart, giving it roots beyond the shallow things of the world and strength for the difficult trials of life, and helps readers to acquire the virtues by witnessing the life of One who possessed each virtue in perfection. These representations are human, deeply tied to Love's own cultural context for good and for ill.

---

7. *Devotional Culture in Late Medieval England and Europe: Diverse Imaginations of Christ's Life*, ed. Stephen Kelly and Ryan Perry (Turnhout, Belgium: Brepols, 2014), contains a wide-ranging collection of essays that traces the many different locations, traditions, and people that this *Meditationes* textual tradition influenced.

8. See Paul Shore, "The *Vita Christi* of Ludolph of Saxony and its Influence on the Spiritual Exercises of Ignatius of Loyola," *Studies in the Spirituality of Jesuits* 30 no. 1 (January 1998), 5–6, https://ejournals.bc.edu/index.php/jesuit/article/view/3970.

9. Shore, "The *Vita Christi*."

10. Love, *Mirror*, 10.

11. Love, 10.

I love his retelling of Christ's nativity. Love describes how Mary, unafflicted by Eve's curse, gave birth without pain, the infant Jesus "suddenly upon the hay" at his mother's feet.[12] She is filled with "sovereign joy," kneeling, taking him in her arms, kissing him over and over.[13] The Holy Spirit teaches her how to nurse the hungry baby God—and as a mother who struggled with nursing, I come close to tears as I feel my kinship with Mary and her Son. The Holy Spirit also leads her to wash Jesus with her milk, breast-milk's antiseptic properties known even then! Mary takes off the kerchief covering her hair and swaddles Jesus in it. The ox and ass take turns breathing on the newborn to keep him warm in the winter's night. As for Mary, "what ghostly riches and inward comfort and joy she had, no tongue may tell."[14] I, the reader, also begin to feel these spiritual riches and inward comfort as I draw close to the Word become flesh and his dear, beautiful, human mother.

Another vivid moment occurs after Jesus's temptations in the desert. Matthew's gospel simply states, "Then the devil left him, and suddenly angels came and waited on him" (Matthew 4:11). Here's how Nicholas Love imagined this scene:

> And then spoke the angels, "Our worthy Lord, you have long fasted, and it is now your time to eat. What should we obtain for you?" And then he said, "Go to my dear mother, and get what matter of meat she has ready. Bring it to me, for there is no bodily food that I like so much as her cooking." And two angels went forth, and suddenly appeared before Mary, and with great reverence greeted her on behalf of her son. And so

---

12. Love, *Mirror*, 38.
13. Love, 38.
14. Love, 39.

the angels took the simple food she had planned for herself and Joseph, with a loaf, and a napkin, and other necessities, and a few small fishes. And the angels came back and spread the towel on the ground and laid the bread thereon, and mildly stood and said grace with our Lord Jesus, awaiting his blessing, and he sat down.

Now, pay attention here, especially you that are solitary. Have in mind, when you eat your food alone without fellowship, the manner of this food, and how lowly our Lord Jesus sits down to his food on the bare ground, for there he had neither table nor cushion. Take heed how courteously and how soberly he takes his food, despite his hunger after his long fast. The angels served him as their lord: one brings his bread, another his wine, another the fishes, and some sing as his entertainment a sweet song of heaven.... This fellowship you have too, though you see it not, when you eat alone in your cell.[15]

This section makes me smile. Details like the divine delivery service, or the angels "mildly standing" and saying grace with our Lord, feel quaint and distant from our own ways of thought. Simultaneously, to think of eating and drinking in the name of Jesus in connection with Christ's temptations presents a theology of joy, of resting and feasting after trial. When you eat or drink alone, you imitate Jesus, and the angels really do accompany you. This message would have been especially encouraging to the Carthusians, Love's monastic order, who lived in community but remained alone and silent for most of the day. They ate alone in their rooms, prayed the liturgy alone, and saw other monks only during times outside their cells. But this devout imagining also

---

15. Love, *Mirror*, 73–74.

becomes a profound comfort to the widow, the impoverished, and the displaced, to anyone who knows the sting of meals shared and now lost to death or separation.

For us postmoderns, the oddest part about this passage may be the emphasis on Christ's excellent table manners. Love connects us to a particular cultural moment. Jesus's courteous conduct identifies him with the most chivalric knight or fastidious lord, despite there being no table and no other guests—not to mention that he had not eaten for weeks on end and most of us would have torn into dry bread with ravenous abandon at that point. Unlike many of these lords, he's not a choosy gourmand; he prefers his mother's simple but delicious cookery to the most angelic fare. This Jesus is a *good medieval Christian*. He is domestic and humble but would fit right in at any glittering medieval court with his well-bred eating habits.

We can also glimpse Jesus the Good Medieval Christian in medieval art. There's a unique manuscript called the Holkham Bible Picture Book. It offers over 230 illustrations of the Old and New Testaments, accompanied by captions in Anglo-Norman French, the language of the ruling class in the fourteenth century. The picture-book Bible was made for teaching and likely commissioned by a Dominican friar in London who wished to increase the biblical literacy of his aristocratic audience.[16] The picture of the Last Supper shows us several details that aren't historically accurate but emphasized important doctrinal beliefs for medieval Christians. On one side, Christ washes Saint Peter's feet in the corner. Peter is tonsured—his hair on the top of his head is shaved—like a medieval cleric. A man of Christ's time would

16. Holkham Bible Picture Book, The British Library, https://www.bl.uk/collection -items/holkham-bible-picture-book.

not have been tonsured, a development of men's "style" that did not happen until the seventh or eighth century, yet the tonsure remains, reminding readers that Saint Peter is the model for all future clerics. Or take a closer look at the Passover meal on the table. It's only round, unleavened circles of bread unpaired with other ancient Middle Eastern foods; it doesn't even really look like bread. It looks exactly like the perfect, white, round host in medieval Mass, emphasizing that Christ is present both in his fleshly body and in his fleshly body that looks like bread. Christ and all his disciples look like white Europeans.

The Last Supper, Holkham Bible Picture Book, manuscript illumination, ca. 1327–1335, Add. MS 47682, fol. 28r, British Library, London.

Album / British Library / Alamy Stock Photo.

Many artists choose to portray Christ as part of their own ethnic or cultural group. Present-day Americans know this well. One famous example from white mid-century America is the famous painting of Christ by Warner Sallman, *Head of Christ*, which is one of the most popular and reproduced artistic renderings of Jesus in history. You recognize it immediately: a blond-haired and blue-eyed Jesus sits at a slight angle, illumined by the studio lighting of an elementary school portrait or the headshot of a moderately successful lawyer. Even the background matches the nondescript, blurred backgrounds of professional and school portraits from the mid-twentieth century all the way to today. This picture does not teach us about the throne of Saint Peter or of the continuity between Christ's historical body and the Eucharist, but it communicates Christ's relevance to white, middle-class America. He's not separate from this world, speaking disembodied from a golden throne in a bejeweled heaven. Salman's portrait emphasizes that Jesus is a human, like us—but which "us"?

Portrayals of white Jesus bring up an obvious problem. The good medieval Jesus or the good mid-twentieth-century white American Jesus can become so firmly aligned with the character and values of only one small subsection of the church at its particular time and place that he no longer bears a resemblance to the second person of the Trinity as the historical Messiah.

Using Jesus the Good Medieval Christian

Often we believe in a Christ too like ourselves, too allied with our present-day concerns and beliefs. If we attentively examine Love's Annunciation, we may notice some strange conclusions about Mary's initial silence when Gabriel comes to her:

> Here then you can take Mary as an example, first to love solitary prayer and departing from humankind so that you may be worthy of the presence of angels. Furthermore, you may take from this to love to hear wisdom, keep silence, and love little speech, for that is a profitable virtue. For Mary heard first the

angels speak twice before she answered them. And therefore, it
is an abominable thing, and great reproof to a maiden or virgin
to be an excessive talker.[17]

Love's interpretation begins with some praiseworthy notes: love
solitary prayer; take time to yourself so that you can become aware
of the charged, divine nature surrounding you. Many of us, especially social media users, would profit from Love's advice to cultivate our love of wisdom and to keep our hot takes to ourselves.

Yet one of Love's takeaways from this holy moment is that
women should keep silent. It's an ironic interpretation, given that
the transformative power of the Annunciation does not come
from Mary's feminine silence. Humankind's participation in
redemption emanates from Mary's vocal consent as a woman to
bearing the Messiah in her womb. Nicholas Love's cultural ideals
of silent womanhood blinded him to the sacred import of Mary's
vibrant voice.

Turning to the Last Supper is even more illustrative of Love's
ideological commitments. In Love's portrayal of the night before
Jesus's death, he focuses on the initiation of the sacrament of the
Eucharist. He describes it with beauty and passion and ends with
conclusions for people to meditate on. Yet it has a polemical edge.

Shortly before Love crafted *Mirror*, a new, radically reforming
theology had sprung up in England, initiated by Oxford theologian John Wycliffe. At the time, Wycliffe and his followers were
called Lollards. Many Lollards proclaimed some controversial,
if not heretical, ideas: that the abundant property of the church
should be confiscated and given to the poor and to the government; the falsehood of transubstantiation, the doctrine that,

---

17. Love, *Mirror*, 25.

at the Eucharist, the host elements became Christ's very blood and sinews, no longer bread or wine; that the church's hierarchy should be abandoned; that women could preach publicly. At first, a few powerful laypeople were drawn to this vision, some from authentic reforming desire, others from a canny realization that they stood to profit from taking away the church's immense property. By the early fifteenth century, the English church hierarchy went into protective mode. England had not burned heretics at the stake, unlike the Continent, but began burning Lollards in 1401, through proclamations by the English parliament and King Henry IV. Ecclesiastical control tightened over which books should be circulating, who could preach, and English translations of holy books. Nicholas Love, aligned with Archbishop Arundel of Canterbury, fiercely opposed Lollardy.

As Love meditates on the Last Supper, he turns specifically to the Lollards, the mix of heretical and heterodox folks of his medieval English church. The true disciples

> left all their bodily reason and wit, and rested only in true belief in their lord's words as said before, save Judas that was reproved for his falseness and unbelief, and therefore he received the blessed sacrament to his damnation.
>
> And so do all that be of his party now, those who falsely believe and say that the holy sacrament of the altar is still bread and wine as it was before the consecration ... they are more reprovable than Judas, for they do not see Jesus's actual body next to the sacrament as he did, and therefore it is easier for them to believe, and more to their damnation.[18]

---

18. Love, *Mirror*, 151.

Mirror contains glosses, mini commentaries, in the margins of the manuscript, inserted by Love himself. These glosses highlight important moments. Love was a careful reader and adapter of the materials of the *Meditationes* and wanted his readers to know when he was extrapolating meaning versus when he was preserving the original material. He had added this section intentionally, and his gloss reads *contra Lollardos*, "against the Lollards." When he depicts the sacrament that unites the church, Love, working with religious authority, weaponizes it.

The Last Supper contains multitudes: the poignant beauty of fellowship in a last shared meal, a theology of fellowship and servanthood, the teaching of the Eucharist, the uneasy calm before the storm of the crucifixion. But in this part of Love's work, this central, powerful, meaningful moment of the Gospels has been weakened into a controlling device for dissidents. *The Mirror of the Blessed Life of Jesus Christ* reveals to us a tendency to picture Jesus as just like ourselves, part of our own culture. It also unveils a devastating and human need to control the Gospels in order to produce a "right" response.

We Are All Nicholas Love

It's easy for us to point a finger at Nicholas Love. Yet we are all Nicholas Love. We all massage our understanding of Jesus in major and slight ways to wield him against perceived threats. The real challenge is identifying when and where.

We are incapable of understanding or interpreting Jesus outside our own time, place, and bodies because of our human limitations. Yet most of us want to impose our version of Jesus on the world, sometimes with good intentions. Nicholas Love was a reformer; he was trying to save his church from what he understood to be dangerous theology. But by using moments like the Annunciation or the Last Supper to control other people, he inadvertently weakened them and enfolded them into humanity's own violent desires.

We are all guilty of fitting Jesus neatly into our culture and our concerns instead of heeding the strangeness of his call. We domesticate him. We think of him like ourselves. Depending on your own background, you probably think of him in your own terms. If you're an American, he tends to become a good American Christian of whatever variety you like best. In my subconscious imagination of Jesus, which I am constantly and unsuccessfully trying to purge, he resembles an open-minded Presbyterian or slightly conservative Episcopalian—he doesn't drink too much but enjoys a glass of wine; he definitely encourages voting, even in his local elections; and he has good table manners as Nicholas Love suggests. He is a mirror of myself. He is less frightening and more understandable that way. I do not consciously think these ideas or express them, as Nicholas Love did. Yet if I am being brutally honest, it's how I feel about Jesus.

Thus, we return to the problem of white Jesus, who all too easily slips from a remembrance that he belongs with people in their ordinary, daily lives to a symbol of white authority.[19] We fail to recognize the contradictions between our cultural values and expectations and the life of the kingdom of heaven. We deceive ourselves into forgetting the burning love and righteousness of the Godhead that prohibits any attempt to use him for our own means.

---

19. Emily McFarlan Miller, "How Jesus Became White—And Why It's Time to Cancel That," *Religion News Service*, June 24, 2020, https://religionnews.com/2020/06/24/how-jesus-became-white-and-why-its-time-to-cancel-that/.

Practices we now find inimical to the life of following Christ have been justified enthusiastically by Christians in history: Forcible conversions for a thousand years in Europe. The Crusades. The slaughter of countless Jewish neighbors by European Christians citing the passion of our Lord.[20] Many Puritan English settlers of North America and Catholic Spanish explorers of South America, despite their very different theology and faith practices, shared the firm conviction of their time and European cultures that Jesus was an ardent colonizer who supported their efforts to gain wealth and land by decimating indigenous people. According to antebellum slaveholders and religious leaders of the American South, Jesus was fully supportive of slavery, specifically slavery predicated on the pseudoscience of Black people as inferior and fitted to the life of enslavement.[21]

Jesus continues to be co-opted to support cultural narratives and control of others. Like many of his predecessors, President Joe Biden invoked scriptural authority, Isaiah 6:8, to justify American military action in Afghanistan.[22] On the news not long ago, I saw a campaign tour bus for a gubernatorial candidate with a massive slogan plastered on the side: "JESUS, GUNS, BABIES." Jesus's name has been diminished to fit a list of "issues" that belong to a particular political party, time, and place. Too often, and most dangerously, we aren't even aware that we are interpreting and

---

20. See David Nirenberg, *Communities of Violence: Persecution of Minorities in the Middle Ages* (Princeton, NJ: Princeton University Press, 1996); Anthony Bale, *Feeling Persecuted: Christians, Jews, and Images of Violence in the Middle Ages* (London: Reaktion, 2010).

21. For a horrifying description of slaveholders' Christian reasoning, see Eugene McCarraher, *The Enchantments of Mammon: How Capitalism Became the Religion of Modernity* (Cambridge, MA: Belknap, 2019), ch. 5.

22. Ed Stetzer, "Don't Confuse Military Action with the Mission of God," *Religion News Service*, August 27, 2021, https://religionnews.com/2021/08/27/biden-isaiah-dont-confuse-a-military-action-with-the-mission-of-god/.

shrinking Jesus, instead believing we are simply reading Scripture as it was meant to be received.

Gazing into the Mirror

The poet John Milton, author of *Paradise Lost*, depicts angels as communicating only through their minds. They have full comprehension of situations and of one another without the intervention of sensory input or corporeal bodies or even space and time—just immediate, full communion while remaining distinct individuals.[23] We, however, are not bodiless, all-encompassing minds (as much as our smartphones may deceive us) but embodied, mortal learners. In other words, we are human. The double-edged gift of being humans is that we are interpreters: of the Bible, of the Holy Spirit, of food and sounds and visions, of one another, of our own opaque desires. Some of the great mystics may have experienced something closer to Milton's angels' total intake of reality and relationship, but not most of us. In humility, in the recognition of our ongoing work of interpretation, and in our status as mortal and embodied, we grow.

If we are not attentive, we will understand our human limitations as a curse. But we know they're not—because God joined us in our full humanity. Jesus calls us into eternal life, love, and humility in our present, time-bound bodies. More paradox: When we imitate Jesus, we become more human, more joyfully cognizant of our frailties, foibles, and beauty. Our increasing humanity leads

---

23. John Milton, "Paradise Lost," pages 283–630 in *The Complete Poetry and Essential Prose of John Milton*, ed. William Kerrigan, John Rumrich, and Stephen M. Fallon (New York: Random House, 2007).

us closer to truth than fruitless attempts to transcend these limitations and become masters of the universe.

In "The Parson's Tale" of his *Canterbury Tales*, Geoffrey Chaucer "englishes" a famous definition of humility from the Latin of Saint Bernard of Clairvaux: "Humility, or meekness, is a virtue through which a man has authentic knowledge of himself, and does not regard himself too highly in regard of what he deserves, but considers ever his weakness."[24] To have authentic knowledge of yourself means you hold your human limitations ever present in your mind. Self-hatred is not humility. Humility is the practice of recognizing and remembering your humanity, your limited capacities for understanding other people and experiences, your body's need for food, drink, and rest, and your natural, blessed dependence on community, without which we would not have the gifts of human friendship or family. The humble person repeatedly confesses how little they understand and listens closely.

"Devout imagination" is not the problem. Often we have too little devout imagination for Jesus's humanity and our own! As we gaze into the mirror of the Christian past, if we can learn to recognize ourselves there, the voices of the dead can speak truth to our present-day power. Love's *Mirror* offers us the gift of clarity—of the stabilizing beauty and encouragement we find when we embrace Christ's humanity instead of the violence we embrace when we make him too much like ourselves. This mirror reflects the curse of our desire for control and the gift of our vulnerability. When recognized and celebrated through humility, the latter is an antidote to the former, not fuel for it.

Thomas Aquinas, following Augustine and the early church

24. Geoffrey Chaucer, "The Parson's Tale," in *The Riverside Chaucer*, ed. Larry D. Benson, 3rd ed. (Boston: Houghton Mifflin, 1987), ll. 287–327.

fathers and mothers, taught that humility, alongside transformative *caritas*—charity, the love of God—was the foundation of the life of virtue.[25] Without our acknowledgment of lack or limitation, no learning, whether playing jazz or practicing justice, is possible. Humility can be delightful or painful. Hearken back to the introduction: For writers like Julian of Norwich, children are examples of humility for adults to emulate. Young children joyfully (and often loudly) request what they need without embarrassment; they are born learners, ready to discover with determined delight what they do not know.

Humility is also a penitential virtue. It is the virtue of self-examination that aids me to recognize where I have been wrong, ignorant, or selfish, where I have acted from scarcity instead of the abundance of life in Christ. In humility, we become more human because we become more like the original exemplar in whose image we are made: the humble God who shares our embodied limitations. Humility is the opposite of control. It is the virtue of the shepherd, of the good mother and father, of the true love, not the dictator or abuser.

As we use Christ's name in violence or vanity, we avoid or outright reject the humanity we share with Jesus and our neighbors, through seeking positions of power, influence, or wealth, via powerful institutions, greater force of arms, attempts to be the most "right," or cultural clout like race or gender. When we claim our limitations and littleness, when we remember we are still growing, as Jesus the Mother reminded us in the last chapter, we become freer. I keep remembering a recent interview with the eminent theologian Stanley Hauerwas in *Plough Quarterly*.

---

25. Thomas Aquinas, *Summa Theologiae*, trans. Laurence Shapcote, ed. John Mortensen and Enrique Alarcon (Lander, WY: Aquinas Institute for the Study of Sacred Doctrine, 2012), II.II.161.5.ad.3.

The interviewer noted that many Christians are concerned about the loss of Christian influence and power in today's America. Hauerwas responded,

> Well, I actually think that one of the good things that is happening today is precisely the loss as Christians of our status and power in the wider society. That loss makes us free. We as Christ's disciples ain't got nothing to lose anymore. That's a great advantage because as a people with nothing to lose, we might as well go ahead and live the way Jesus wants us to. We don't have to be in control or be tempted to use the means of control. We can once again, like the first Christians, be known as that people that don't bullshit the world.[26]

This is important: Christianity's loss of social status, of cultural power and currency to guard and defend ferociously, is a secret gift of freedom. We can finally recognize that it is not we who move hearts, but the Holy Spirit—and sometimes we are given the gift of participation in that movement. I can be honest within the blessing of the guide rails of the Creeds and Scripture about how much remains a mystery to us even in our faith: suffering, death, war, the promise that, in Julian of Norwich's words, "all shall be well."[27] When we practice humility, there will be less control and more repentance. There will also be less fear. Fewer promises we cannot keep; less power that does not rightfully belong to us. To borrow from Hauerwas: less bullshit.

---

26. Stanley Hauerwas, "Peacemaking Is Political: An Interview with Stanley Hauerwas by Charles E. Moore," *Plough Quarterly*, March 16, 2021, https://www.plough .com/en/topics/justice/nonviolence/peacemaking-is-political.

27. *The Writings of Julian of Norwich: A Vision Showed to a Devout Woman and A Revelation of Love*, ed. Nicholas Watson and Jacqueline Jenkins (University Park: Pennsylvania State University Press, 2006), 27.10.

So, Nicholas Love teaches me. Christians have lived and always will live in this tension as followers of Jesus—that Christ is like us, but we must not use that likeness for our own ends. We remember and draw the truth out in our devout imaginations: Jesus is like me, he bled like me, cried like me, had a grieving mother and good friends. He speaks to me through material gifts in his creation, through books and birds and the joy of my children. He loved his mother's cooking. Maybe he had immaculate table manners. He's not like Zeus, disguising himself as a man to seduce someone yet still possessing all the powers of his divinity. Though Christ ate with angels in Love's narrative, the food was made by his mother with her own hands. His impoverished mother wrapped his funny-shaped newborn body in her own headscarf. Jesus was hungry and thirsty, weak and tired.

As the Lord often graciously works, our weaknesses end up revealing truth. The woman has herself painted into the Annunciation in an act of showing off; she inadvertently ends up pulling back the curtain on something deeper, her participation in salvation history, her belongingness with the incarnate God. I am the woman in the Annunciation: miraculously part of salvation history through the gift of shared human vulnerability with the immanent Godhead. You are too.

Meditation and Practices Inspired by the Good Medieval Christian

- Meditate on Paul's famous verses and hymn from Philippians on the mystery of God becoming man and its effect on how we understand ourselves and act in the world. What stands out to you?

Do nothing from selfish ambition or empty conceit, but in humility regard others as better than yourselves. Let each of you look not to your own interests but to the interests of others. Let the same mind be in you that was in Christ Jesus,

who, though he existed in the form of God,
did not regard equality with God
as something to be grasped,
but emptied himself,
taking the form of a slave,
assuming human likeness.
And being found in appearance as a human,
he humbled himself
and became obedient to the point of death—
even death on a cross.

Therefore God exalted him even more highly
and gave him the name
that is above every other name,
so that at the name given to Jesus
every knee should bend,
in heaven and on earth and under the earth,
and every tongue should confess
that Jesus Christ is Lord,
to the glory of God the Father.

Therefore, my beloved, just as you have always obeyed me, not only in my presence but much more now in my absence, work on your own salvation with fear and trembling, for it is God who is at work in you, enabling you both to will and to work for his good pleasure. (Phil. 2:3–13)

- How have you fit Jesus into a neat cultural box of your own making? How have you used Jesus to control others, in politics, in relationships? Identify these thoughts and actions and confess them to someone you love and trust.
- Spend some time with Christian writing or art from a different time than your own. The nineteenth century can be just as helpful and challenging as the fifth century, and fiction is just as useful as theology, so whatever interests you: Augustine or Austen, Douglass or Ignatius (or all of the above). How do the faithful and imperfect people of the past domesticize or instrumentalize Jesus for their own purposes? How does their insight into Jesus challenge you?

Prayer

Jesus, fully human and fully God, I ask that you speak to me wherever I am, through means I can notice. Help me to pay attention to you. Help me to gaze into the mirror of the past, of my brothers and sisters in Christ, so that I may discover the ways I have twisted your gospel and humanity to better match my own expectations and desires right now. Lead me to discern where I am trying to control others by invoking you. Give me the gifts of humility and repentance, and give me the power and strength to relinquish that control.

Jesus, true God and true man, I thank you for joining me fully in my human limitations. I thank you for coming as a baby who cried, experienced cold, and happily nursed. I thank you that I am not alone when I eat, sleep, think, and work. I thank you for the gifts of my body and my mind and all their beautiful and challenging limits. Help me to remember these good gifts and rejoice in them. Amen.

Chapter Eight

The Wounded God

In one of the stranger metaphors of the Middle Ages, Christ's crucified body is a document, sometimes a book or a charter. Inspired by vellum, the animal skin on which words were written, medieval thinkers saw Christ's broken body as a charter crafted by compassion, and the strange hieroglyphs of his streaming blood as the contract in which we are united to him. The fourteenth-century English hermit Richard Rolle wrote,

> Sweet Jesus, thy body is like a book written all with red ink; so is thy body all written with red wounds. Now, sweet Jesus, grant me to read that book, and somewhat to understand the sweetness of that writing, and to enjoy studious in-dwelling of that reading. And give me grace to catch a glimpse of the peerless love of Jesus Christ, and to learn by his example to love

God as I should. Grant me this study in each moment of the
day . . . ever to be my meditation, my speech, and my dalliance.[1]

What did this book of anguish tell medieval people? Gazing at
Christ's wounds in art or their own imagination was part of the
cure and comfort of the crucifixion. Reading the body also meant
directly confronting Christ's afflictions and understanding his
pain—and ours too—as a place of union.

We have met the suffering Jesus in many of the preceding
chapters already, in different guises—the Mother giving birth in
agony to the church; the Knight come to fight without shield or
spear; the Lover offering his wounds as conjugal home; the Judge
showing his pierced hands and feet as a reminder of his mercy and
justice. But now here we are, to read the red ink for ourselves.

Facing the Discomfort

In the passion, if we truly look at the face of Jesus, we come unavoid-
ably face-to-face with human pain. Medieval people were less afraid
of this than we are. They boldly asked, "Was the suffering on the
cross necessary?" "What does suffering do?" And perhaps most
controversially, "How should I share in Christ's sufferings?"

The church had not always asked these particular questions
around the passion. As you may remember from the "Judge"
chapter, early crucifix representations reflected the awareness that
the God-man on the cross was still the ruler of the universe, fully
divine even in his humiliation. In the later Middle Ages, culture

---

1. Richard Rolle, *Meditations on the Passion*, in *English Writings of Richard Rolle
Hermit of Hampole*, ed. Hope Emily Allen (Oxford: Clarendon, 1931), 36, lightly translated by myself.

and theology both began to change, as always, influencing one another. The crucifix, called a "rood," became the most popular representation of Jesus in churches, often displayed above or to the side of the altar. One of the most influential theories of atonement, taught by Saint Anselm of Canterbury, concentrated on Christ's humanity; artists too began to attend to his humanity and thus his pain and suffering.[2] Perhaps prompted by terrible wars over succession, the ongoing reign of the Black Death, and the dueling popes in Avignon and Rome for almost a century, medieval people believed there had to be some redemptive value in suffering, through identification with Christ or imitation of his pains. Sometimes this striving for imitation took the form of severe purgation or penance. This was the age of the hair shirt, the *stigmata* (wounds in the hands and feet given by God to medieval saints like Saint Francis of Assisi that echoed the wounds of Jesus), and self-flagellation. Sometimes this compassionate suffering was more about the emotional response to Christ on the cross: the gift of weeping, or "roaring," in the words of Margery Kempe; pilgrimage to be bodily present to holiness in the form of relics; intense affective responses of love in what scholars today call "affective piety." Often these different practices and attitudes overlapped.

---

2. Many theologians and historians have speculated on the reasons for this transformation. One theory is that explanations of atonement were changing: theologians like Saint Anselm of Canterbury and Peter Abelard were postulating different theories on why Christ died on the cross and how this death was salvific. Anselm's satisfaction theory and Abelard's sign of love were hotly debated in monasteries and the burgeoning universities of the eleventh and twelfth centuries. Simultaneously, big pastoral changes were taking place. The sacrament of penance and the instruction of laypeople in doctrine had both become more important. If you'd like to learn more, see Denise N. Baker, *Julian of Norwich's Showings: From Vision to Book* (Princeton, NJ: Princeton University Press, 1994), ch. 1; Rachel Fulton Brown, *From Judgment to Passion: Devotion to Christ and the Virgin Mary, 800–1200* (New York: Columbia University Press, 2002); Ellen Ross, *The Grief of God: Images of the Suffering Jesus in Late Medieval England* (Oxford: Oxford University Press, 1997); Richard Vilaseau, *The Beauty of the Cross: The Passion of Christ in Theology and the Arts, from the Catacombs to the Eve of the Renaissance* (Oxford: Oxford University Press, 2006).

I immediately have some objections to this intense focus on suffering as our way into thinking about the cross and union with Jesus. The first is practical: How can suffering be a place of union? Pain is weirdly individual. Though writhing around, mentally or physically, is concrete and real in your own experience, you have never felt another person's pain, and they have never felt yours. Suffering is profoundly isolating because no one can fully understand your hurt. When I gave birth to each of my children, I always hated when the doctors and nurses would ask me where I was on the pain scale of one to ten. One time, probably on a drug, I politely asked the nurse if a ten was like being disemboweled in a public execution (once a medievalist, always a medievalist). How are we supposed to rate our pain when we have no idea how anything feels for anyone else? Loneliness and suffering often go hand in hand.

The second objection is instinctual: ick. I have no desire to glorify unnecessary suffering. Placing a lot of value on suffering has been used in the past to justify some really bad things, like continuing the mistreatment of oppressed people and staying in abusive relationships. At the hands of patriarchal society, suffering in love was overemphasized for certain groups, which turned patience, submission, and humility into specifically feminine virtues, forced and not chosen, instead of Christian virtues.[3] In the medieval era, bursts of anti-Semitic violence sprouted like weeds fertilized by the emotional response to martyrdom and passion narratives.[4] In some

3. See, for instance, Beth Allison Barr, *The Making of Biblical Womanhood: How the Subjugation of Women Became Gospel Truth* (Grand Rapids: Brazos, 2021), for an account of Christian confusion over oppression and suffering itself as godly for women (and people of color as well, though that's not the central point of the book).

4. Chaucer's "Prioress's Tale" in his *Canterbury Tales* is an example of the hideous, *extremely* popular, anti-Semitic genre of miracle stories, sometimes called blood libels, in which children are killed by Jewish people, miracles of the Virgin, Eucharist, or Passion occur to expose the murder/murderers, then Christians slaughter their Jewish neighbors.

parts of medieval Europe, violence toward the Jews became connected specifically to Holy Week, part of an unholy "liturgy" avenging Christ's death.[5]

However, I'm also deeply cognizant that one of the biggest differences between medieval people and myself is that while they may glorify suffering to a fault, I see in it only cause for dread and avoidance. No culture has spent more time and effort avoiding suffering than my white, middle-class American culture—and perhaps all Americans in general. We are collectively terrified of it; we do not know what to do with it. Our avoidance ranges from the most mundane to the most universal life moments, from the tedious, extremely minor suffering of waiting at the DMV to the universal suffering of aging and dying that we hide with style or surgery or sequester to nursing homes and funeral parlors.[6] The unafflicted sometimes treat those with chronic pain or the grief-stricken as though they have the plague—we mustn't get too close, or else we might catch the pain or loss ourselves. There's a whole class of billionaires dedicated to "solving" death.[7]

With these fears and burdens in mind, might there be a strange, hidden wisdom waiting for us postmodern folk in reading the book of Christ's suffering alongside medieval people?

---

5. See David Nirenberg, *Communities of Violence: Persecution of Minorities in the Middle Ages* (Princeton, NJ: Princeton University Press, 1996), ch. 7, on the ritualized killing of Jews during Holy Week in France, Italy, and Spain, often explicitly encouraged by religious authorities. One example from Spain during Holy Thursday services: "Children would shake their rattles and sing . . . 'Marrano Jews: you killed God, now we kill you.'" Such singing often erupted into violence, riots, and murder (202).

6. For a thoughtful book on suffering in our suffering-avoidant society, see K.J. Ramsey, *This Too Shall Last: Finding Grace When Suffering Lingers* (Grand Rapids: Zondervan, 2020).

7. Cf. Ariana Eunjung Cha, "Tech Titans' Latest Project: Defy Death," *Washington Post*, April 4, 2015, https://www.washingtonpost.com/sf/national/2015/04/04/tech -titans-latest-project-defy-death/.

Beholding the Cross

Julian of Norwich begins her *Showings* by describing three striking petitions she made to God in her youth. In the first, Julian
requests to have more "feeling" in the passion of Christ, to see
"bodily" his suffering alongside Mary Magdalene and other lovers of Christ, to suffer with him as did those who loved him.[8] In
other words, she does not want some kind of mystical, pleasurable
ravishment of Christ's pain; she wants to really see the full horror,
to feel the dread, devastation, and compassion felt by the women
at the foot of the cross, and to identify with Jesus, his weeping
mother, and one of his best friends. The second request is to suffer
a "bodily sickness" that would nearly bring her to death to aid her
in purging herself of attachment to things not Christ.[9] These first
two requests she asks conditionally, unsure if they are the will of
God. The last, unconditional appeal is for three "wounds" in her
life: "the wound of true contrition, the wound of kind compassion,
and the wound of willful longing to God."[10] Julian is praying for
pain—spiritual, physical, and emotional suffering.

If a friend confessed that this is what they were praying,
I would probably recommend that they visit a good therapist.
Julian's requests are puzzling and alarming to us in modernity.
Why would Julian want a "bodily sight" instead of just imagining
the scene, as many of her contemporaries did? What did it mean to
gaze at the cross? How did one feel, and why did it matter?

Many medieval lyric poems of the era envisioned Jesus as
speaking to the passersby at the foot of the cross. Christ issues

---

8. *The Writings of Julian of Norwich: A Vision Showed to a Devout Woman and
A Revelation of Love*, ed. Nicholas Watson and Jacqueline Jenkins (University Park:
Pennsylvania State University Press, 2006), 2.5–8.

9. *Writings of Julian of Norwich*, 2.18.

10. *Writings of Julian of Norwich*, 2.34–36.

a challenge or invitation to them. What are they going to do in response to beholding his wounds? An Easter sermon of the day uses one of these lyrics. Imagine the priest giving his homily with the crucifix in plain sight. This crucifix implicitly echoes the poem: a Jesus who "crieth" and "sayeth" the message of the cross each day, visible and familiar to parishioners:

> Listen, man, listen to me,
> Behold what I suffer for thee.
> To thee, man, well loud I cry;
> For thy love thou seest I die.
> Behold my body how I am hung
> See the nails how I am through stung
> My body without is beaten sore
> My pains within be far more.
> All this I have suffered for thee.
> As thou shall at Doomsday see.[11]

In gazing at the crucifix, in imagining Christ speaking to them thus, viewers were encouraged to meditate on their complicity in the passion in their sinfulness. They were also encouraged to respond with compassion, with identification with Christ's humanity in his suffering. Taken alone, though, the sermonic poem makes me feel a bit like when someone asks me a leading question about my emotional state: Aren't you *just so sad*? Sometimes medieval affective piety makes me feel guilty that I'm not sadder.

An early crucifixion painting (ca. 1420–1423) from the masterful Fra Angelico clarifies the stakes. Our responses to this

---

11. *Speculum Sacerdotale: Edited from British Museum MS. Additional 36791*, ed. Edward H. Weatherly (London: Published for the Early English Text Society, Oxford University Press, 1936), 112.

extreme suffering aren't just about feelings. Fra Angelico's crucifixion more artfully asks the same thing the poem does in the sermon: How will you respond in the face of Christ's suffering? The painting has a unique composition.[12] Christ dies on the cross at the very center, surrounded by a semicircle of onlookers. Blood from Christ's wounded hands drips down his corpse-pale arms, slipping off into the golden background. Blood from Christ's wounded feet trickles down the wood of the cross and pools on the bare earth. Though he is central, he is slightly turned away from the viewer at an almost experimental angle.

Fra Angelico, *The Crucifixion*, tempera on wood, gold ground, ca. 1420–1423, Metropolitan Museum of Art, New York.

Public Domain.

---

12. The Met's website has an excellent description of this painting's influences and origin, accessed June 28, 2022, https://www.metmuseum.org/art/collection/search/437007.

Our attention is drawn toward the circular arrangement of observers. Soldiers sit on magnificent warhorses, chatting with one another, casual in the presence of pain and gore. Some, with callous curiosity but no emotion, glance up at the Savior. Some look bored; some contemptuous. Religious leaders converse in the background, on their own horses. Some soldiers and bystanders even look straight up in aghast confusion and wonder.

And then there's a group of five people at the front, emblazoned with haloes. Mother Mary, swooning in agony, feels the prophesied sword piercing her soul.[13] The other women, their faces intent, eyes red with weeping, tend to her in different postures. Saint John, at the right of the cross, cannot look at Jesus; he clutches his hands together in an expression of disbelief and deep sorrow as he bows his head toward the blood on the ground. We recall that the other disciples were too frightened to show up at all. As we look at Fra Angelico's crowd, we realize we too are onlookers, alongside Mary, Mary Magdalene, John, and the casual, careless soldiers and leaders. The vast array of attitudes prompts me: Where do I fit within the array of perspectives, feelings, and responses?

Fra Angelico reminds us that these observers are witnesses. To witness the humiliation and anguish of another asks for a response from us. We feel sorrow, which can give rise to two important responses: contrition and compassion. As scholar Ellen Ross has noted, the sorrow provoked by the passion is "curative."[14] When I regret how I have hurt someone, when I have learned to weep over the ways I wound myself and others, it helps me and the other person to heal. Such sorrow belongs to the broad penitential tradition

---

13. Luke 2:35.
14. Ross, *Grief of God*, 10.

that was so important in the late medieval era. To be vulnerably exposed to the pain that our sin has wrought, to seek out true knowledge of how we have hurt each other, of how God himself has suffered for our transgressions—this feeling of acute regret and remorse is called contrition.

Observing the callousness of the soldiers and leaders also reminds me of all the times I have seen suffering and turned away, ignored it, justified it, or distracted myself with happier thoughts and conversations. I have lacked compassion. Julian's request for a bodily sight so she may weep next to Mary Magdalene and Mary the mother of Jesus belongs to her desire to expand her imagination of what it means to love God. Suffering alongside Christ is, curiously, a way into that expansion by way of compassion. Famously, the etymology of *compassion* reveals its core: *com-pati* means to suffer with. The cross becomes a site of a "great oning," quite literally oneing, between Christ and ourselves because when we love someone, we suffer when they are hurting.[15] It is because of their friendship with Jesus that Christ's friends suffer and are drawn near to him when they or he suffers.

This shape of human friendship is natural; it is inherent to our created humanity. It is what medieval people would have called *kinde* (keen-deh). It's an important word for Julian: she notes that in our present lives and in gazing at the cross, "we are in disease and labor with him, as our nature [*kinde*] asks of us."[16] It's fitting that Julian calls her last prayer request three "wounds": "the wound of true contrition, the wound of kind [*kinde*] compassion, and the wound of willful longing to God."[17]

---

15. *Writings of Julian of Norwich*, 18.10–14.
16. *Writings of Julian of Norwich*, 21.21.
17. *Writings of Julian of Norwich*, 2.34–36.

For Julian, suffering for love is a "kinde" act. *Kinde* is a Middle English word deeply layered with significance. *Kinde* is an ancestor of our modern English *kind*, a meaning that it encompasses but goes beyond. It also means natural, inherent, part of our created being. When we refuse to acknowledge suffering, to share in each other's trials, to weep with those who weep, we deny our very being. Compassion is human, *kinde*. The callous rejection of others' suffering is *unkinde*, unkind and unnatural to our calling as people who "weep with," people who "rejoice with." Sin is *unkinde*.

When we do not look away from the cross, when we face the devastation of our actions, the violence of the world, the terrible grief of loss, we become more human, more kind, more fully ourselves. By his wounds we are healed, says the prophet (Isa. 53:5). Our own wounds of contrition and compassion as we gaze at him paradoxically play a part in this healing.

Yet cultivating responses of contrition and compassion is not the ultimate lesson of the medieval cross. Julian unearths more wealth to be had in gazing at the crucified Son of Man.

The Great Sign of Love

At the tail end of the medieval era, Matthias Grünewald (ca. 1470–1528) created the justly famous, riveting altarpiece at Isenheim in present-day France. It is a massive piece, with Christ on the cross looking close to life-size. If you thought Fra Angelico was graphic, Grünewald is overwhelming. This Christ is in agony. His fingers curl and flex torturously around the nails embedded in his palms. Mother Mary swoons in John's arms, paler than the white clothes she wears, deathlike in the ravages of her grief. Mary Magdalene's own fingers, as she clasps them in prayer, take on the same shape of suffering as Jesus's, flexing too in bodily, catastrophic pain. Jesus's face is turned slightly away as his head droops. He is on the verge of death. The crown of thorns, unruly, scrapes his neck. His lips look dried out; he thirsts.

Matthias Grünewald, *The Crucifixion*, Isenheim Altarpiece,
mixed media (oil and tempera) on limewood panels,
ca. 1512–1516, Musée Unterlinden, Colmar.

If we look closely, we notice that Christ's body is covered with realistic sores. They almost pass for the wounds from the scourging, but they look distinctively like a skin disease. In the entombment below the passion (not included in the image), it's even more obvious. The sickening, irritated scabs cover his thighs and arms. But Grünewald's gruesome crucifixion is not indulging in some sort of pointless glorification of suffering or sadism. This altarpiece was painted for the monastery of St. Anthony at Isenheim. The monks of St. Anthony had a hospital that cared for plague victims and those suffering from skin afflictions like leprosy. In the medieval era, as in Jesus's time, lepers were social outcasts. They were sometimes, like Jewish people, accused of poisoning others, persecuted, and even killed.[18] Their condition was not only painful but humiliating. Jesus's marks on his body look remarkably like those often smelly and socially questionable ailments. He is an object of disgust and fear according to the mores of the time. In that place of bodily agony and humiliation, sick people saw the God who looked like them, who dwelt among them, who took on their individual, horrifying afflictions. Grünewald's Christ spoke to the suffering, ill men of St. Anthony's hospital: "I suffer like you. I suffer with you. I suffer for you." He was there in the depths of Sheol (Ps. 139:8). And these men, haunted by rotting limbs and plague sores, in return profoundly identified with Christ. They recognized him in themselves and recognized themselves in him. So it is not just we who have compassion on the living God—in his death he has compassion on us, suffering with all who suffer, in any and every variety of pain.

Jesus told Julian in her mind, "If I could suffer more, I would suffer more."[19] She is deeply comforted by what she understands as utmost assurance of his love. In a reading group I led once, the readers struggled with this idea. What would be the point of Christ suffering *more*? Why did Julian take so much comfort in Christ's statement?

---

18. Nirenberg, *Communities of Violence*, ch. 4.
19. *Writings of Julian of Norwich*, 22.4–5.

Take a breath and seriously consider this staggering assumption of all suffering into himself. I suffered prenatal depression with my oldest daughter and another bout of depression and anxiety after the birth of my youngest. Both times I blamed myself and was ashamed of my inner turmoil. How dare I feel so sad in the face of the sheer gifts of love that were my infant daughters and when I had a loving husband, a cozy home, and supportive friends and family? I knew this shame was equally wrong because what was happening was the response of my hormone-sensitive body and not something I had control over. Still, I wasn't able to reason myself into health. I told my husband it felt like two versions of me lived inside my brain: regular Grace, who recognized reality, and pregnant/nursing Grace, who lived in weird, untethered sorrow. That sorrow was like an endless staircase with no windows, winding down into depths of darkness. My husband, though deeply supportive of me, could not understand what I felt and thought.

When I understand Julian's Jesus saying, "If I could suffer more for you, I would suffer more for you," when I see Grünewald's leprous Christ, I see in Jesus one who knew exactly what my prenatal depression felt like, who was there in the winding dark staircase with me. This perspective I have gained only in retrospect, with the God-given aids of Zoloft, sleep, and time. But now I can't stop seeing it when I gaze upon the cross. I see communion there. Alongside skin conditions or prenatal depression, Christ suffers poverty, abuse, prejudice, rejection, violence, all illness. As Julian said, love would not let him stop taking our pains on himself.

This is the miracle of being "oned" with Jesus in the cross—there is someone who has taken into himself every pain, as Grünewald knew well. Grünewald's painting communicates that we aren't the only ones who feel compassion; *Jesus* feels compassion and deep love as he suffers with us in the worst moments of our lives.

The Bliss of the Cross

"The Bliss of the Cross" is an interesting heading. One would be forgiven for thinking it is a missed typo. Surely *Resurrection* should take the place of *Cross*. But surprisingly, bliss is where we end up in Julian's visions of the passion.

Julian watches Jesus die for a long time. One of the worst aspects of her witness to his pain is that Jesus dries out as he dies, his wounds becoming progressively more painful—aching, gaping. She repents of her request to witness his death; she expects that death to come at any moment. But his face suddenly changes. His wounded, dried-out countenance becomes "blissful." Julian, surprised, suddenly too becomes "glad and merry."[20] He tells Julian, "It is a joy, a bliss, an endless liking to me that ever I suffered the Passion for thee."[21] It is as if Julian not only suddenly experiences the gore and blood of witnessing the passion on earth but also unexpectedly sees it cosmically.

The self-giving work of the passion is a joy for the Godhead. Julian associates a word with each person of the Trinity. The "Father is pleased, the son is worshipped, the holy ghost liketh," says Julian. The horrid work of the cross, including the suffering, is a labor of love in which God delights. Catholic theologian Frederick Christian Bauerschmidt writes, "The Trinity, like the cross, is a pure self-giving in love; unlike the cross, however, it is unmarred by the suffering and violence that human sin imposes. Its only labor is the joyful labor of delight."[22]

---

20. *Writings of Julian of Norwich*, 21.9–10.

21. *Writings of Julian of Norwich*, 22.3–5.

22. Frederick Christian Bauerschmidt, *The Love That Is God: An Invitation to Christian Faith* (Grand Rapids: Eerdmans, 2020), 41.

There's a popular, almost dreamlike motif in medieval art called the "throne of grace" or the "seat of mercy." It metaphorically portrays the Trinity together in the passion—a large God the Father gently holds a little Christ on the cross in his hands, and the Holy Spirit as a dove flutters above the Son's agonized head. Without minimizing Jesus's suffering, it emphasizes the holy unity

Laurent Girardin, *The Trinity*, oil on wood, ca. 1460,
Cleveland Museum of Art, Cleveland.

Public Domain.

of salvation, the eternal joy that exists alongside the temporary bodily pain. For me, it brings back the inadequacy of my human efforts to get at this central mystery of sacrifice through simple explanations. But what's left, what's clear in the throne of grace, is the utter fulfillment of love.

As Saint Bernard of Clairvaux wrote, "The more surely you know yourself loved, the easier you will find it to love in return."[23] Says the medieval Christ on the cross: You are loved. You are loved. You are loved. It is a joy, a bliss, an endless liking to me to express my love to you in all ways you can receive it, even when you try to avoid love or even kill it.

The World within the Wounds

Julian's third prayer for unconventional wounds—wounds of true contrition, *kinde* compassion, and willful longing to God—speaks to me in a new way after meditating on the passion. It still feels weird to call them wounds, but wounds they are. To love is to carry wounds (both your own and others'), to remain vulnerable and open. To keep your conscience aware and active in the midst of your reactive drive for self-justification (contrition), to hold your heart open to the pain of loving others in a broken world (compassion), to remain grateful for though fundamentally unsatisfied with the things of the world and cultivate longing for the fulfilling grace and goodness of God (willful longing)—these are wounds that will not heal in the present life.

In our pilgrimage to become more *kinde*, embracing our

23. Bernard of Clairvaux, *Song of Songs I*, 154 in *Opera* vols. 1 and 2, *Sermones super Cantica Canticorum*, ed. Jean Leclercq, C. H. Talbot, and H. M. Rochais (Rome: Editiones Cistercienses, 1975–1958); found in Baker, *Julian of Norwich's Showings*, 59.

created selves, becoming more like Jesus, Julian recognizes that we imitate Christ on the cross through these wounds. We do not need to follow any of our medieval forebears in self-flagellation or starvation in attempts to get closer to Jesus. We do not need to punish or despise ourselves for sin and weakness. Asking for these wounds and keeping them open is hard enough. Praying for this gift means resisting the constant temptation to harden myself into a personal citadel of safe isolation in a society that attacks vulnerability and avoids people in pain. This will look different for every person.

The thought of keeping myself vulnerable, open, *kinde* scares me. But the idea of open wounds reminds me of something else. I grew up in Phoenix, Arizona. The Sonoran Desert is one of the most wildly beautiful places on earth, but you have to learn to appreciate that beauty. The desert is out to get you, from spiky cacti that love to cling to your clothes, to rattlesnakes warning you not to come too close, to the eternally beating sun that can kill even in winter. If you're ever on a walk in the Sonoran Desert, you may come across an odd object that looks a bit like a boot. It's actually a remnant of a long-dead saguaro cactus.

When the cactus was alive, birds like Gila woodpeckers and gilded flickers drilled holes into the living, fleshy membrane of the massive giant. Other than the spiny skin of the cactus, the holes are mushy, but over a year or so, the cactus transforms each of them into waterproof negative space inside itself by drying out the tissue around it and secreting a special sap that encases it and creates scar tissue. Many different birds, with magical names like elf owls and purple martins, build safe, waterproof, even fairly temperature-controlled nests inside these desert kings.[24] The great saguaro's

---

24. For pictures of the birds and creatures living in or among the saguaros, see "Wildlife Interactions with Saguaros," National Parks Service, accessed July 1, 2022, https://www.nps.gov/sagu/learn/nature/saguaros_animals.htm.

wounds have become homes for the small and tender ones of the desert. Once the saguaro dies, this "boot," that hardened scar tissue nest, is the last thing to disappear, becoming, instead of a hole inside the cactus, a shape on the desert floor. It's all that remains of the giants that can grow to seventy feet tall, live for hundreds of years, and weigh over a ton: a tangible reminder of wounds transformed into life-giving space for another creature—*kinde* wounds.[25]

There is a world within the wounds. Recall the image of Christ the Lover, where Christ's side wound becomes a "nest," a haven for the hungry, yearning, unloved soul. The saguaro is what I have learned to think of—hope for—when I follow my medieval friends to meditate on the wounds of Jesus and request the wounds of contrition, compassion, and longing. We are made like both the saguaro and the birds of the Sonoran Desert. Imitating the Wounded God means letting our own open wounds—our vulnerability and humility through our compassion, ready contrition, and open yearning for Jesus—become havens for our fellow pilgrims in the wilderness. And like elf owls, we flee to his wounds as succor in the desert places. Jesus the saguaro.

Meditation and Practices Inspired by the Wounded God

- Meditate on Isaiah 53:3–7:

> He was despised and rejected by others;
> a man of suffering and acquainted with infirmity,

---

25. For the facts on saguaros, see "Plant Fact Sheet: Saguaro Cactus," Arizona-Sonora Desert Museum, accessed March 10, 2023, https://www.desertmuseum.org/kids/oz/long-fact-sheets/Saguaro%20Cactus.php.

and as one from whom others hide their faces
    he was despised, and we held him of
        no account.

Surely he has borne our infirmities
    and carried our diseases,
yet we accounted him stricken,
    struck down by God, and afflicted.
But he was wounded for our transgressions,
    crushed for our iniquities;
upon him was the punishment that made us whole,
    and by his bruises we are healed.
All we like sheep have gone astray;
    we have all turned to our own way,
and the LORD has laid on him
    the iniquity of us all.

He was oppressed, and he was afflicted,
    yet he did not open his mouth;
like a lamb that is led to the slaughter
    and like a sheep that before its shearers
        is silent,
    so he did not open his mouth.

- Read the account of the crucifixion in any one of the gospels: Matthew 26:36–27:65; Mark 14:32–15:47; Luke 22:39–23:56; John 18:1–19:42. Sit with it. Pray for attention to the suffering Jesus.
- Gaze upon some of the images of the crucifixion and Christ's wounds for a period of quiet contemplation, from five minutes to half an hour, whatever you have time for.

What stands out? How do you feel, what do you think, what strikes you as you stand under the cross just like Fra Angelico's observers?

Prayer

In the fifteenth century a nun named Margery Byrkenhed collected this humble, heartfelt prayer for her community of nuns in Chester. Oxford scholar Eleanor Parker suggests that the repetition of *Jesus* in some lines of medieval prayers works as a breath prayer. You might like to inhale and exhale deeply with each repetition of his name.[26]

Oh Jesus, let me never forget your blessed passion,
That you suffered for my transgression.
For in your blessed wounds is the true school
That must teach me by the world to be called a fool.
Oh Jesus, Jesus, Jesus, grant that I may love you so,
That the wisdom of the world may clean from me go,
And may I burningly desire to come see your face
In whom is all my comfort, joy, and solace.
Amen.[27]

26. Eleanor Parker's blog first brought Margery Byrkenhed to my attention: "Two Medieval Prayers to Christ," *A Clerk of Oxford* (blog), August 16, 2013, https://aclerkofox-ford.blogspot.com/2013/08/two-medieval-prayers-to-christ.html.

27. From *Religious Lyrics of the XVth Century*, ed. Carleton Brown (Oxford: Clarendon Press, 1939), 28, lightly translated by myself.

Conclusion

Jesus as Us

If anyone ever asked me if I have a favorite medieval feast day—an extremely unlikely scenario, I know—the answer would be yes. Not counting Christmas (my favorite feast day of all time), it's the feast of Corpus Christi, the midsummer celebration of the Body of Christ (in Latin, *Corpus Christi*) that especially honors the Eucharist. Some branches of Christianity still celebrate it, though often under a different name.[1]

In the Middle Ages, the Eucharist was the center of corporate worship and often controversy.[2] The feast of Corpus Christi celebrated the doctrine that when the priest consecrated the bread and wine at Mass, it was no longer bread and wine at all, merely the appearance of bread and wine. What looked like bread and

---

1. In the modern Roman Catholic Church, this feast is officially celebrated as the Solemnity of the Most Holy Body and Blood of Christ. Some Anglican and Lutheran churches observe it as well, sometimes under the name Thanksgiving for Holy Communion.

2. To read about the language and theology around the Eucharist and the mystical Body of Christ in the Middle Ages, see Henri Cardinal de Lubac, SJ, *Corpus Mysticum: The Eucharist and the Church in the Middle Ages*, trans. Gemma Simmonds, CJ, with Richard Price and Christopher Stephens (Notre Dame, IN: University of Notre Dame Press, 2006). For the doctrinal history and development of the feast day, see Miri Rubin, *Corpus Christi: The Eucharist in Late Medieval Culture* (Cambridge: Cambridge University Press, 1991).

wine was actually the very blood, sinews, muscle, and flesh of Jesus Christ, the eternal but one-time sacrifice that redeems and unites Christians in our mortal bodies. For most medieval Christians (and many Christians today), Communion was not symbolic or an act of remembrance but an active consumption of the real body of Jesus.

Procession for Corpus Christi, Master of James IV of Scotland, manuscript illustration, ca. 1510–1520, MS Ludwig IX 18 (83. ML.114), fol. 48v, Getty Museum, Los Angeles.

Gibon Art / Alamy Stock Photo.

At first, processions commemorated the occasion, with the consecrated host, the Body, looking like a small white cake ensconced in an often magnificent monstrance, blessing the viewers and participants everywhere it went. Then, perhaps inspired by the pageantry and joy of those processions, cities and villages added outdoor plays to the festivities. As you might recall from chapter 2, in towns like York, Coventry, Chester, and others, guilds of different tradespeople and artisans theatrically depicted the Bible, from creation to Revelation. The content of the play rather charmingly (at times grimly) determined the guild in charge of it. For example, the "fysshers and marynars," fishermen and sailors, put on "The Flood" at York. More soberly, the "shermen," the folk who sheared cloth, performed "The Road to Calvary," in an echo of the sheep sheared before slaughter. The "pynneres," the makers of pins and nails, and the painters depicted the raising of the cross. The butchers, who had access to a lot of blood, aptly put on the mortification and burial of Christ.[3] The point is that ordinary, working people embodied the events of Scripture, right in front of your face.

Corpus Christi mystery plays concretized the wild idea that we humans, in our very different bodies and vocations right here and right now, are Christ's body on earth. Christ was not only in the monstrance, the beautiful glass holder of his Body in the guise of bread. If you had been an actor, perhaps your friend was Jesus on the cross, your enemy was Jesus teaching in the temple, or your uncle was Jesus harrowing hell. And at the same time, you were the one who drove the nails into Jesus, or John the Baptist baptizing him. The body of Christ in God's broken earthly kingdom of

---

3. Read more about how these plays were put on in Clifford Davidson's introduction to *The York Corpus Christi Plays* (Kalamazoo, MI: Medieval Institute, 2011), 1–13.

fifteenth-century York reenacted the saga of Christ and his body in first-century Palestine. Through their strange literality, these plays reminded their viewers of the past and now remind readers of the present that you are Corpus Christi and so am I. Our different jobs, bodies, and lives creatively reflect different moments, aspects, and truths of Christ's redemptive ministry.

Let it sink in. *We* are the last face of Jesus in this book.

The down-home implications of this idea are beautiful and alarming. They filter into every part of our lives. There's the obvious thought: what a different world it would be if my fellow Christians and I learned to see the face of Jesus in other people, as they were, in all ragged obscurity. What if we were better at discerning Christ in the ill, weary, and oppressed? In the annoying and the stupid as well as the wise and good? And among those categories, there's also myself. It's hard to believe I am literally part of Jesus. Yes, I know Paul's words in Romans, Ephesians, Colossians, and Corinthians, but somehow I tend to spiritualize those words or defer them.[4]

Medieval Christians took this idea seriously whether or not they celebrated the feast of Corpus Christi. The Lollards did not believe in the real presence of Jesus in the Eucharist and would not have celebrated a holy day like Corpus Christi. Hear the witness of a fifteenth-century Lollard woman named Margery Baxter explaining to a neighbor why she did not adore the crucifix or the Eucharist. In a small medieval cottage, Baxter had thrown out her arms expansively, in an imitation of Jesus on the cross. Standing in the dim, firelit room, arms rigidly, ecstatically raised, she announced, "This is the true cross of Christ, and you ought and can see and adore that cross every day here in your

---

4. Romans 12:4–5; Ephesians 4:16; Colossians 1:18; 1 Corinthians 12:12–31.

own house."⁵ Baxter was not referring to herself explicitly, like many tragic would-be prophets. She took our status as the body of Christ as seriously as the worshipers and players on Corpus Christi did. They disagreed on what was happening in the sacrament, yet they were united in the belief that, miraculously, our own bodies and those of our fellow Christians are the body of Christ in front of our own eyes.

Surely the hidden playwrights of York, Margery Baxter, or Paul himself could not mean that I, Grace Hamman, and you, just as we are, are Christ's body? Yet they did. This idea is not new, and many mighty lovers of God have written about it again and again. In the early days of the church, Origen, meditating on ministering to the spiritually afflicted, wrote, "When we visit a brother sick either in faith or in good works, with doctrine, reproof, or comfort, we visit Christ himself."⁶ Saint Vincent de Paul, in the seventeenth century, urged the newly founded Sisters of Charity to leave off their personal prayers and go to the spiritually or materially needy if they heard of someone in desperate straits: in doing so, they "leave God for God."⁷ Dietrich Bonhoeffer, resisting Nazism in the twentieth century, wrote, "The Church is not a religious community of worshippers but is Christ himself who has taken form among men."⁸ And famously, Mother Teresa of Calcutta, in an acceptance address for the Templeton Prize, said,

5. *Heresy Trials in the Diocese of Norwich, 1428–31*, ed. Norman P. Tanner (London: Royal Historical Society, 1977), 44.

6. Origen in St. Thomas Aquinas, *Catena Aurea: Commentary on the Four Gospels*, vol. 1, *St. Matthew*, trans. John Henry Newman (London: John Henry Parker, J. G. F., and J. Rivington, 1841), 872.

7. St. Vincent de Paul, *Correspondence, Conferences, Documents*, vol. 13b, ed. Sr. John Marie Poole, trans. Sr. Helen Marie Law, DC, Sr. John Marie Poole, DC, Rev. James R. King, CM, Rev. Francis Germovnik, CM, from the 1920 edition of Pierre Coste, CM, and annotated by Rev. John W. Carven, CM (New York: New City Press, 1985), 138.

8. Dietrich Bonhoeffer, *Ethics*, ed. Eberhard Bethge (London, United Kingdom: Touchstone, 1995), 84.

We are touching His body, it is the hungry Christ that we are feeding, it is the naked Christ that we are clothing, it is the homeless Christ that we are giving shelter, and it is not only just hunger for bread, and nakedness for clothes, and homelessness for a house made of bricks, but Christ today is hungry in our poor people, and even in the rich, for love, for being cared for, for being wanted, for having someone to call their own.[9]

Our own faces are a face of Jesus I am still learning how to love.

This book has been a school of love. Some of these metaphors, images, and ideas of Jesus I already knew and loved. Some I had a hard time connecting with and chose to write about only because they were important to medieval people. For almost every chapter, I would start with just airing my often quite valid hang-ups and concerns and suspicions about the particular face of Jesus sometimes beautifully rendered and sometimes rudely sketched by my medieval brothers and sisters. Yet even the ones I was originally most intimidated by (the Judge) or most skeptical of (the Lover) ended up speaking profoundly to me about Christ's character. I offer only a sample of the Jesus metaphors the medieval church used.[10] Like catching a piece of a reflection in a broken mirror, each representation catches and renders an aspect of a Christ bigger, more beautiful, more glorious than any of them could separately communicate.

Here is what I am learning in this school of love:

---

9. Mother Teresa of Calcutta, "Acceptance Address for the Templeton Prize," April 24, 1973, https://www.templetonprize.org/laureate-sub/address-of-mother-teresa-of-calcutta/.

10. I could have also written about the Shepherd, the Vine, the Baby, and more. Additionally, each of these chapters includes only a small portion of the many ways that the version of Jesus within was portrayed.

To long for the return of the Judge; to become a just and
merciful neighbor right now.

To yearn for the adoring and fiery union with the Lover; to
welcome the change that Love will make in me.

To hope and rejoice in the courage of the Knight; to be
formed in his fortitude in life's struggles large and little.

To ask questions and speak boldly about the Word; to
discover and embrace where my words fall short.

To run to my Mother in all my hurt and need; to realize I am
his beloved child.

To celebrate the blessed humanity of Christ; to confess how I
use him and remake him in my own image.

To witness Christ's sufferings with me and for my sake; to
bear my own cross of *kinde* wounds.

To learn how to see Jesus in the lovers, fighters, justice
workers, sufferers, mothers, teachers, children, fools, and
wonderfully embodied humans made in his image. In
the words of the nineteenth-century Jesuit poet Gerard
Manley Hopkins, "Christ plays in ten thousand places, /
Lovely in limbs, and lovely in eyes not his / To the Father
through the features of men's faces."[11]

11. Gerard Manley Hopkins, "As Kingfishers Catch Fire," in *Poems by Gerard Manley Hopkins*, ed. Robert Bridges (London: Humphrey Milford, 1918), 54.